Fetch

Fetch

Train your dog with
fun *and* **games**

Pippa Mattinson

EBURY
PRESS

1

Published in 2025 by Ebury Press, an imprint of Ebury Publishing
Penguin Random House UK
One Embassy Gardens, 8 Viaduct Gardens,
Nine Elms, London SW11 7BW

Ebury Press is part of the Penguin Random House group of companies
whose addresses can be found at global.penguinrandomhouse.com

Design: Clare Sivell
Production: Percie Bridgwater
Publishing Director: Elizabeth Bond
Project Editor: Fionn Hargreaves

First published by Ebury Press in 2025
www.penguin.co.uk

A CIP catalogue record for this book
is available from the British Library

ISBN 9781529909173

Printed and bound in China by C&C Offset Printing Co., Ltd.

The authorised representative in the EEA is Penguin Random House Ireland,
Morrison Chambers, 32 Nassau Street, Dublin D02 YH68.

Penguin Random House is committed to a sustainable future for
our business, our readers and our planet. This book is made
from Forest Stewardship Council® certified paper.

Contents

Introduction

What if I were to tell you that there is a way to fill your dog's life with immense joy and keep them in superb physical condition without going for a two-hour walk every day? What if I told you that this 'way' could be taught in not much more than a few minutes each day and would make your dog utterly focused on you? And how about if I told you that this 'way' would also give you a means to exercise your dog under control in public places and spaces. And if I also mentioned that this 'way' would bring you great pleasure and pride in your dog. Would that interest you?

Retrieving *is* the way. And retrieving is not just for retrievers. It's a brilliant form of entertainment for all dogs. It's also one of the best forms of controlled exercise available to dogs anywhere in the world. The purpose of this book is to show you how to teach your dog to fetch reliably on your command, any time, anywhere. And you'll learn how to do it without using any force at all – no discipline, no cross words, no cajoling, pushing or pulling. The process is quite involved, but it's great fun. You will learn to teach your dog to fetch like a pro using a series of short and simple games.

I want it to be clear that any breed of dog, no matter what their heritage or genes, can learn to retrieve, so I decided to photograph and film this process, not with one of my retrievers, but with my husband's Jack Russell terrier, Polly. And it is mainly Polly's journey to becoming a 'retriever' that we follow through this book.

Polly was born on Christmas Eve 2019 and we brought her home just as the world was waking up to the Covid pandemic. As a lockdown puppy she is a little shy but she's also a lot of fun. And I hope she will help to dispel the myth that you can't teach an old dog new tricks!

Playing fetch is a great alternative to free running exercise for dogs with

Polly as a puppy

strong hunting instincts, that are distractible or that engage in inappropriate chasing. It is also a great starter course for hunting companions, including retrievers, spaniels and versatile hunt point retrievers, such as vizslas and weimaraners. If you are training a retriever for the shooting field, you should know that this course does not include advanced retrieving techniques, such as complex directional control and whistle stops. But it does lay a foundation on which you can build those techniques and avoids you making most of the common beginners' mistakes that can cost you time and put your dog off the whole retrieving process.

There are six training stages to this book. Each stage takes you a step closer to being part of an awesome team with your dog! Before we start training, we'll look at what you will need in the way of information and equipment and I'll explain how the games work and how to get the best from them. The first chapter of this book looks at what separates dogs that won't fetch, or that quickly get bored of fetching, from dogs that love to fetch and do it with style. We'll need to understand the instincts that lurk beneath the surface of every puppy and underpin the desire to retrieve. And we'll look at how dogs were (and still are) trained to retrieve using traditional methods, and how the methods you'll be using in this course are very different.

I hope *Fetch* inspires you to have a go at teaching your dog to retrieve. I believe that retrieving is so beneficial to dogs that every dog should have a chance to learn this fantastic and entertaining skill. This book goes far beyond a simple game that a dog and their human can play together; it teaches you the fundamental principles that underpin all dog training and gives you a powerful way to train your dog without force or intimidation. If you finish this retrieving course with your dog, by the end of it, you, too, will have acquired an amazing bonus. You'll have a set of skills that will enable you to teach your dog pretty much anything of which they are physically capable. And I can't wait to get you started!

Preparation

The dog should make it easy for you to take the toy

How retrieving works

At first glance, retrieving – or 'fetch' – appears to be a simple game. You throw a toy and your dog fetches it and returns it to you. But not all dogs know how to play in a way that really brings the game to life. Many dogs will briefly chase a ball or stick but lose interest once it stops moving. Some dogs will collect the ball then run off with it, while others will return with the toy but refuse to hand it over. Then there are dogs that have little interest in chasing anything, ever, and dogs that only want the toy so that they can destroy it in record time. Interestingly, all these dogs can be taught to retrieve a toy and deliver it into your hand so that you can throw it again. Which is of course the essence of a game of fetch, and the only way to make the game fun for all the players!

Getting this basic level retrieve established is what this book is about, but a simple game of fetch isn't just a lot of fun for you and your dog, it is an incredible tool on which to build a wide range of activities that exercise not only your dog's body but also its mind.

Who can play?

Most healthy adult dogs will benefit from retrieving, but like any other form of exercise, you need to build up the intensity gradually over time. Young puppies should not be exercised hard and it's a good idea to wait until teething is over, at around seven months, before embarking on this course. If you have a brachycephalic (flat-faced) dog, such as a pug or bulldog, they may struggle with any kind of exercise, especially in warm weather. And so it would be sensible to have a chat to your vet before progressing to outdoor activities. The same applies to elderly dogs or those with health conditions that might affect their ability to exercise.

The benefits of retrieving

While the game of fetch can be as simple as picking up a ball and returning it at your feet, retrieving can be very complicated indeed. The games you can play, and the skills your dog can gain, once they understand the concept of fetching and delivering a toy, are extensive. Advanced retrievers can be stopped and directed by whistles and hand signals at distances of a hundred yards or more, enabling them to find hidden objects in partnership with their human handler. They gain skills that include patience, focus, tracking, persistence, problem-solving, and the ability to follow advanced cues, such as stop, left and right. Retrieving sharpens recall, massively improves attention and the ability to ignore distractions, and is a wonderful, bonding experience. Best of all, fetch is a game that almost every dog has the ability to play at some level and it helps keep them fit.

Of course, there's a reason that many dogs and their owners never get to experience the joy of retrieving. Even in its most basic form, fetch is a complex chain of behaviours rather than a single action. There are many components of a retrieve, which means that there are many ways for it to go wrong! And without knowledge or experience, it can be hard to put things right. This book is a detailed course in basic retrieving for all dogs and its purpose is to give you the knowledge you need to master the basics of this highly rewarding game. You don't need to worry about the experience side of things, you'll gain plenty of that as you work through the book.

At first glance, fetch appears to be a simple game, but not all dogs know how to play

Can any dog retrieve?

When pet dog owners come up against a challenge while playing fetch, they tend to assume that their dog is simply not a natural retriever and give up. In fact, all dogs of every breed or breed mix have some retrieving instinct. The desire to retrieve is part and parcel of a dog's original role as a predator and hunter of other animals. And the ability to catch and kill is dependent on the predatory sequence of chasing, grabbing and carrying food. Most dogs enjoy at least some parts of that sequence immensely. And all breeds and types of dog capable of carrying a small toy in their mouth can be taught to retrieve.

That doesn't mean teaching fetch is easy. But it is within the grasp of most dogs. We'll look at training methods in more detail in a moment. First let's deconstruct the retrieve and find out exactly what we're up against.

The components of fetch

Below are the components of fetch in the order that the dog carries them out. It's not the order in which we teach these components, and in a moment, I'll explain why that is. During a perfect trained retrieve, a dog does the following:

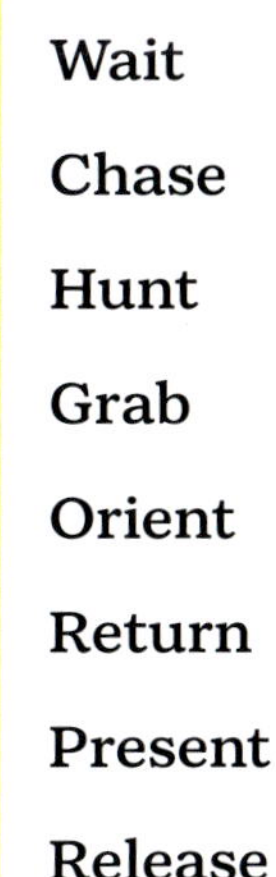

Mark

Wait

Chase

Hunt

Grab

Orient

Return

Present

Release

1. The mark

Marking is the part where your dog watches to see where its ball or toy lands after you have thrown it and estimates how far it needs to travel to get to the landing zone. Marking is harder than you might think. It's surprisingly difficult to judge accurately where a small item has landed. You can test this yourself by throwing a tennis ball into some long grass. It's even harder for a dog, as you have the advantage of being several feet taller. Now try getting a friend to walk fifty yards away from you and throw the ball. The further the area of fall, the harder it is to accurately pinpoint the landing spot.

Many dogs are pretty good at judging the distance and location of a falling object but really accurate marking is part natural ability and part training or experience, which means that all dogs can improve with practice. The better your dog is at marking, the more likely they are to be able to run out in a straight line from you to the toy. This means a faster, more efficient retrieve; and fewer lost toys!

It's also possible to play fetch games that don't involve marking at all. You can hide a toy when the dog isn't looking, for example, and dogs can be taught to seek out the hidden toy on your cue or command. Retrieves that don't involve marking are called 'blind retrieves'.

2. The wait

Retrieving is exciting, yet waiting for permission to chase is vital in hunting dogs, and a useful skill in pet dogs that play fetch around other dogs. Several dogs all headed for the same retrieve can end up in fights, and a dog that dashes after a moving target without permission is at risk of chasing wild animals, birds, joggers and even traffic. This is why I'll show you how to teach your dog to retrieve on your cue and not before. Retriever trainers call this ability to wait for a cue before chasing a retrieve 'steadiness'. The benefits of lessons in steadiness include a level of canine self-control that will spill over into other aspects of life with your dog.

3. The chase

Chasing is brilliant fun for most dogs, but there are some dogs that have no interest in pursuing a ball or toy at all. Often because they have been put off retrieving by some common mistakes that you won't be making if you follow the system in this book. And sometimes because fetching has never been motivating for them. We'll be fixing that problem quite early in this process.

4. The hunt

Hunting is when the dog uses their nose to sniff out a toy they cannot see. The ability and desire to hunt are another link in this chain that is strongly influenced by breeding and instincts. Hunting can be an important part of playing fetch, because if the ball you just threw lands in some long grass, the dog won't be able to see it once it stops moving.

Inexperienced dogs give up quite quickly if they can't find the ball, but we can teach dogs to hunt and not give up looking until they find their toy, using their amazing sense of smell. This persistence in hunting is developed by ensuring lots of early success and introducing more challenging retrieves gradually.

5. The grab

Perhaps surprisingly, it's quite common to find dogs that chase after a ball with huge enthusiasm, but will not pick it up. This is pretty frustrating for you and means that the dog misses out on a lot of fun. Chasing after a moving object is very exciting but for some dogs, the chase starts to lose its appeal when the object stops moving. The trained retrieve you are about to teach your dog overcomes this issue by teaching the pick-up *before* adding the excitement of the chase.

6. The orient

Retrieving is a team effort. The first thought of the dog that has successfully found and picked up a retrieve should be *where is my partner?* (that's you!). In order to complete a successful fetch from a distance, your dog must identify your position and orient itself towards you. They must not be thinking about chewing up the toy or engaging the toy in a game by themselves. This is where a solid method of training becomes so important. In the trained retrieve, the orient is 'attached' to the return so that the two automatically follow in sequence.

7. The return

Some trainers use a recall whistle once the dog has picked up the toy both to encourage the orient and to trigger the return. With the method you will learn here, the return will be automatic. You won't need to call your dog, unless they are having trouble finding you.

8. The present

This final part of the retrieve, the part where the dog delivers the toy into your hand, is one of the most prone to error. Presenting the toy means that the dog lifts up their head and makes it easy for you to take the toy in your hand. With an untrained retrieve, many dogs will return with a toy, then duck away from the handler's hands because they don't really want to let go of it. Using the methods in this book, your dog will always choose to offer you the toy on their return because it's what they have been taught from the beginning.

9. The release

The delivery isn't over when the dog presents you with the toy. It's only over when you give the dog a cue to let go of the toy. Releasing the toy is extremely difficult for many dogs, so choosing and using this cue correctly is an important part of the retrieving process and one that we get going on right away.

Step by step

As you can see, the retrieving business is not as simple as teaching your dog to sit. But that's okay because I'll be taking you step by step through the whole process. And I want to reassure you that you do not need to be an experienced dog trainer to succeed at this. Nor do you need previous experience of force-free training; just an enthusiastic interest in spending time with your dog and a willingness to learn.

Different dogs

Every dog is different and when we put the links in the retrieving chain together, there will still be some dogs that excel more at different stages of this process. Some puppies are blessed with retrieving instincts in a supercharged form. These tend to be puppies from breeds that have been bred to retrieve in challenging conditions over generations – breeds such as labrador retrievers, golden retrievers, German short-haired pointers, cocker spaniels and English springer spaniels.

We often refer to these supercharged instincts as 'drive' because they power the dog forwards, even in the face of difficulties. Some dogs have enormous drive to hunt with their noses and you'll be able to develop this aspect of their personality with games that include retrieves that are increasingly difficult to find. Other dogs are hugely driven to run fast and furiously over long distances and you'll be able to harness that enthusiasm with longer retrieves and games that help you control the dog at a distance. Some dogs are more inclined to be couch potatoes and may need you to continue to provide motivation for them to play fetch. Many find the games so motivating that the opportunity to play becomes its own reward. All these different dogs can learn to love the game of fetch.

Natural drive

Natural retrieving drive can be enhanced or depleted by experience. All puppies will have their chasing and grabbing instincts changed and shaped by the environment in which they grow and develop. A puppy that often has toys snatched from its mouth by other dogs or children may soon lose interest in chasing and carrying stuff, for example. And the same applies to a puppy that is reprimanded for stealing the TV remote or your favourite socks. Even mild punishments (such as a scolding) when a puppy is holding an object can inhibit the puppy from carrying anything in its mouth at all. The less 'drive' that a puppy has to begin with, the quicker it can be snuffed out by unrewarding experiences. And it used to be thought that once quashed, the retrieving drive could never be recovered.

Training methods have changed

As more people train the retrieve using modern force-free techniques, it is becoming clear that some of the old beliefs are simply not true. With the use of modern training methods, it is possible to rekindle the joy of retrieving in dogs that have learned not to love it. And even to kindle a love of retrieving in dogs that have never shown any interest in it at all.

The transition from traditional to effective modern methods in the dog training community is a relatively recent one and is in large part the reason I am able to teach you how to train your dog to retrieve through a series of enjoyable games. In the next chapters we'll be looking at the principles and techniques that govern how dogs learn and, more specifically, at how fetch can be taught not just to dogs that have generations of retrieving ancestors lined up behind them, but to any dog whose owner enjoys playing with them.

Training principles

In this chapter I'm going to set out some training principles that will guide you as you work your way through this book. We'll start by looking at what makes dogs do the things they do and how you can influence the choices they make by reinforcing the choices you approve of. I'll also consider how the bad choices your dog makes might accidentally be reinforced and how you can avoid that happening.

Reinforcement vs reward

The words reinforcement and reward are often used interchangeably, but they are subtly different. Reinforcement is a behavioural term defined by its effects on the dog's behaviour. Reinforcement is something that changes behaviour, and if it doesn't change behaviour, it isn't a reinforcement. A reward on the other hand is something we give in recognition of an action we approve of. But not all rewards are reinforcing, even if they are intended to be! Whether or not a reward changes behaviour depends on the quality of the reward. And dogs and people often differ in what they regard as rewarding. Many people struggle with dog training because they are using rewards that are *not* reinforcing for their dog. As a result, many dogs find being around their owners largely unrewarding, while finding other activities very rewarding indeed!

In fact, what is rewarding differs from one dog to another in just the same way as I might be happy to run around the block in return for a box of chocolates, while you might only be tempted to do so in return for a T-bone steak. It's all about personal taste. All dogs find food reinforcing, unless they have eaten recently, but some foods are more reinforcing than others. Some dogs find praise and petting mildly reinforcing while many do not. What you need to remember is that if the rewards you choose for your dog do not change the dog's behaviour in any way, then they are not reinforcements. And if you want your dog's behaviour to change, it is reinforcement that you need.

Beware the environment

Although the early training in this book begins indoors, playing fetch is largely an outdoor pursuit. It is important to remember that the environment has the potential to provide enormous reinforcement for all dogs. And it is environmental reinforcement that results in the all-too common problem of 'selective hearing' where your dog only obeys your commands when they feel like it. For most dogs, the outdoor environment has been the most generous and reliable provider of reinforcement for much of their lives, providing them with endless opportunities to sniff, run and chase. Dogs are born with powerful desires to do these things, so we ignore those desires at our peril.

Outdoors there are scent trails to follow, leaves blowing in the wind, a mouse scuttling through a hedgerow, seagulls on a shoreline, other dogs at the park. These are all ever-changing, and highly reinforcing for a dog. With this kind of reinforcement history, why should your dog be interested in you? The answer lies in the way you manage the dog's access to the reinforcement that is so richly provided by the environment. And in the way you actively provide reinforcement to your dog, by playing games that fulfil those powerful desires to sniff, run and chase. This is of course, where fetch comes in.

Modern training, including the course in this book, is based on the principles of reinforcing desirable behaviours with powerful rewards, *combined* with management techniques to prevent the environment becoming your worst enemy. Modern training also generally avoids the use of force, so it's important to understand why that is.

Learning how to pay attention and please you are wonderful by-products of fetch training

Punishment and force

In the past trainers would try to compete with the environment by punishing dogs for failing to respond to their commands. This is a challenging approach once a dog is off-leash, because punishing a dog at a distance requires that you first catch your dog, which is not an easy task for many of us. And while you are thinking up ways to trick, corner or catch your dog, the environment is thinking up new and more interesting ways to draw their attention away from you and reinforce them for ignoring you.

Aside from the ethical debates powering the movement towards kinder methods of dog training, there are significant downsides to training with force or intimidation. Several studies have shown that training using punishment, even mild forms of punishment, increases aggression in dogs. This is a very real concern for owners of large and powerful dogs; it also causes dogs to 'shut down' and stop trying, which makes it hard to teach dogs new behaviours.

Modern training starts by teaching your dog that you are astonishingly rewarding to be around and to pay attention to. It introduces the distractions of the environment gradually as the dog becomes more and more focused on their relationship with you. At the heart of this concept is the principle that choosing to do what *you* want gets the dog what *they* want.

Choosing to please you

All well-trained dogs have something in common. They understand that the best way to get what they want is to please their human partner. This does not come naturally to a dog. A dog's natural instinct when they see something that they want, is to try to get it for themselves.

If you place a piece of meat under a wire cage in front of a hungry, untrained dog they will do their level best to get at the meat using their paws and teeth. A trained dog will look at their human companion and try to figure out what behaviour they need to offer their human partner, in order to be *given* the meat. The gulf between the dog that thinks it has to provide its own solution and the dog that knows that *you* will provide the solution is vast. Fortunately, that can be changed quite quickly and this new mindset is not only easy to teach, it's also a game-changer when it comes to training because it puts you in control of the training process. Watching your dog learn how to make good choices is part and parcel of this course and will stand you in great stead when it comes to teaching your dog a whole range of other skills.

Playing fetch is enormous fun but better still, retrieve training is the most powerful way of competing with environmental reinforcement and of fulfilling all those amazing urges to sniff, run and chase that mean so much to your dog. It can enable you to have your dog off-leash without losing control of it and without being outdone by all those environmental distractions that lead so many dog owners to tear their hair out. In other words, you'll have a dog that listens!

In the next chapter we'll look at the training techniques that you'll be using as you learn to play fetch with your dog.

Training techniques

Retrieving methods have changed significantly over the last few decades and these changes have helped to open up the world of retrieving to a much wider community of dog owners. Traditional retriever trainers use a variety of methods to 'hone' their retrievers' natural instincts into a useful and controllable behaviour. But many of these trainers use techniques, facilities or a level of skill not easily acquired or available to the average dog owner.

Traditional methods nurture natural instincts rather than creating new behaviours from scratch. And as we have seen, these instincts can easily be squashed by inexperienced trainers' inadvertent mistakes. So both modern pet dog trainers and some traditional retriever trainers have looked for ways to standardise retriever training and to make the process more reliable and less dependent on natural ability in either dogs or their human partners. In doing so, two very different approaches have evolved. One of those approaches involves force; the other does not.

Force-fetch

The use of the forced retrieve, or 'force-fetch', was developed in the USA within the working retriever community where it has now become mainstream. Force-fetch involves applying pain to some part of the dog's anatomy, usually an ear or a toe, and then ending that pain when the dog complies with the trainer by taking the retrieve object into their mouth. This overcomes the problem of the dog that won't pick up a toy and prepares the dog for e-collar training. Later the ear pinch or toe hitch is replaced by an electric shock delivered from an e-collar, which enables the trainer to use the concept of forcing the dog forwards on to the retrieve, even at a distance.

Force-free

While trainers in the hunting dog community were refining the use of negative reinforcement using e-collars, some trainers in the agility and obedience training community were going another way and developing the force-free retrieve. It was to this community that I turned when I wanted to find a training method that did not use pain, and that would tackle some of the challenges and inconsistencies of developing my dogs' natural retrieving instincts. I wanted a method that would ensure all my young dogs learned to retrieve effectively and reliably, while at the same time having a lot of fun.

Teaching a trained retrieve some 20 years ago was my first real experience of force-free training and I enjoyed it so much and was so impressed with the results that I began to transition to using force-free methods with all my dogs across a whole range of different skills. If you are still using traditional training methods, I really hope that these games inspire you to do the same.

The importance of shaping

If you ever see a dog carrying out a complex task you are most likely witnessing the results of shaping. Shaping is a simple but powerful behavioural modification technique. Modern trainers use shaping to teach dogs to carry out behaviours that do not come naturally to them, or to build chains of complex behaviours. And we'll be using shaping to get exactly the results we want with our fetch training programme.

With shaping, we reward a dog for an action that they can easily achieve. We keep on delivering rewards each time the dog performs the action, until the dog knows what we are looking for and is enthusiastically offering the behaviour over and over again. We then stop rewarding that action and wait for the dog to offer something different. You know what you are looking for, but your dog has to figure it out. For example, if you want a dog to bump something twice with their nose, you'll start by reinforcing them for touching it once. Then you'll stop rewarding them while they figure out what comes next. They'll try harder bumps and double bumps. And you'll start rewarding the double bumps. And the more you train with your dog the quicker they will start to offer new and interesting behaviours each time the flow of rewards is switched off. Once they pick the behaviour you want, you start rewarding them again, until you are ready to challenge them to offer an even better behaviour.

Shaping allows us to create and reward a finished behaviour that we might otherwise wait a long time for a dog to carry out. And it's a vital part of the trained retrieve. In our fetch games we use shaping to teach a dog to interact with the fetch toy in various ways. This is science-based training in action, and the skill lies in knowing when to move the goalposts and what you can reasonably ask for next. You'll have this skill nailed down by the time you finish this course.

Marking the behaviours we like

An important component of shaping is event marking. We need to identify for the dog the exact point at which they carry out an action that we like. This action could be something as simple as touching your hand with their nose or touching a toy with a paw. And to mark that action, we usually use an audible signal, such as a click.

Dogs are lively and quick and may carry out many actions in rapid succession, so, we need to be quick too, in order to capture the exact behaviour we are going to reinforce. This is especially true with retrieve training where in some of our games, we mark quite small changes in behaviour. Event marking avoids any confusion about what the reward is for and there are various types of event marker. I'll go into that in a bit more detail in the next chapter. But first let's take a closer look at how we control those rewards.

Providing and controlling reinforcement

When we are training, we try to make sure that reinforcement comes in the form of a reward that *we* deliver to the dog, such as a treat or game of tug, and not from the environment. We've talked about environmental reinforcement and it's important to be aware that reinforcement can sometimes be hard to control.

Dogs do get better at ignoring distractions outdoors each time they succeed in doing so. This means that to begin with you need to engineer that success by setting things up so that the dog can win. That means managing their access to distractions and training in a small, distraction-free area, until the skills required for that game become second nature. If your dog is distractible in your garden, then you'll play with the dog on a training leash (long line) to begin with.

Until a dog has reached the point in the retrieving process when the act of fetching becomes intrinsically rewarding, we need to find a way to motivate the dog to play our game. Choosing the right rewards is important. Later on, when your dog has developed a passion for retrieving, we'll often use the opportunity for *another* retrieve as the reward for this one. But to begin with we'll be using food to reinforce your dog's behaviour. Every time your dog hears your marker, you'll immediately give them a tiny treat. We'll talk a bit more about using and preparing treats in the next chapter.

It's important to choose the right rewards to get the games started

Adding cues

In traditional training, cues are often referred to as commands, and they are given to the dog at the beginning of the training process, before the dog understands what they mean. For example, we used to say 'sit' to a dog, then press down on the dog's butt and pull up on their collar until the dog was in the sitting position. Over time the dog came to learn to sit on hearing the word 'sit', in order to avoid being pulled about. There are downsides to these kinds of traditional techniques. Dogs tend to resist physical pressure and if you push down on a dog's rear end they instinctively push back. If you say 'sit' at the same time, they associate the word 'sit' with pushing upwards. This delays the dog's understanding of the real meaning of the word.

In modern training, the cue is added towards the end of the early training process, when we have shaped the behaviour and fine-tuned it a bit. Later we add distractions to the training process to consolidate the dog's understanding that sit always means sit. Later still, we teach the dog to discriminate between different cues.

In essence the cue is a label for an action that the dog already knows. Once the label is attached to the behaviour the cue can be used to initiate that behaviour. So, if you are excited to reach the point where you say the word 'fetch' to your dog, be patient. It will come. We are going to get the behaviour right first, so that we don't attach our very important label (cue) to the wrong set of actions, or to a half-baked behaviour sequence.

The cues we give our dog when playing fetch are all verbal ones, so you don't need to buy a whistle. In fact, the equipment needed for retrieve training is fairly minimal but there are a few things you'll need to assemble or prepare, so we'll look at those in the next chapter.

Training equipment

You'll need just a few items to get started with teaching your dog to fetch: a toy to retrieve, some treats, a container for your treats and a marker to let your dog know when they are winning!

Many different types of toy can be used to play fetch. Traditionally, trainers from different disciplines or dog sports have used specific types of toy to train their dogs and have given them special names. Gundog trainers in the UK tend to call their fetch toys 'retrieving dummies'. In the USA, the word 'bumper' is common. And in obedience circles, a 'retrieving dumbbell' may be more familiar. If you prefer to use a regular toy, that's fine, you'll be able to switch later if you want to.

There are some key differences between your dog's fetch toy and any other toys they may have. The most important difference is that the retrieving toy belongs to you and you'll always have control of it. You'll bring it out at the start of each game and put it away at the end. It's very important that you don't let your dog have access to this toy at any time other than during training, so you need to have a place to keep it safe and out of your dog's reach.

The right fetch toy

The right fetch toy for your dog is a toy that they will enjoy picking up and holding. With this method, it doesn't matter if the dog isn't very interested in the toy to begin with, but it's helpful if it's not a toy that your dog is completely obsessed with and desperate to possess. The tricky part is that you won't necessarily know whether you have chosen the right toy to begin with and occasionally it's necessary to switch one toy out for another one. I'll let you know if and when you reach that point. Just be prepared to be flexible about your choice of toy and willing to experiment.

The weight of the toy you choose can be important. It shouldn't be so light that you can't throw it very far, nor so heavy that your dog struggles to lift it. The Kong goody bone is a good choice and comes in three different sizes. The size that you'll see our terrier Polly carrying is a medium. The toy is bigger at each end than in the middle, which is helpful as it encourages the dog to grasp the toy in the centre. Your chosen toy also needs to be long enough that you can take hold of one end while the dog is still carrying it.

I would avoid cuddly toys or toys that squeak at this point, as they encourage the dog to chomp on the toy, instead of gripping it with a calm, still mouth. This is especially important if you are planning to move on to gundog work later. In this case, you might want to consider a purpose-made retrieving dummy. These come in many different styles and colours, including white, which is easier for the dog to see outdoors. My gundog training dummies are made by Dokken and are available from gundog suppliers online in the UK and USA.

The retrieving dummy will be easier for the dog to see outdoors

Event markers

We talked briefly about marking behaviours in the previous chapter. During the shaping process, your dog may sometimes carry out other behaviours too, such as barking or jumping up at you. We therefore need a way to let the dog know what action we are rewarding them for, and to isolate it from any other behaviours that are happening around it. The tool we use for this is called an event marker. An event marker is a signal, usually a sound, that tells your dog they are on the right track. Event markers are very powerful. It's like saying,'Hey! I liked it when you did *that.*' Event markers gain their power through being paired with reinforcement. The dog will know you liked what it did, because you will pair the event marker with a reward. The marker identifies for the dog exactly what you liked, what you are willing to pay for and, therefore, what you want him to do more of. There are two simple event markers for you to choose from.

Clicks and words

The most common event markers used in dog training are clicks and words. A popular event marker is the 'clicker', a small plastic or metal box, with a flexible plate or button in the centre that makes a clicking sound when pressed. It's also possible to use your voice as an event marker. Words such as 'good' or 'yes' are popular. Some people prefer to train with a verbal event marker, and this does have the benefit of leaving both your hands free. But, apart from the first lesson of this training course, I recommend you use a click from a clicker rather than a word. And there are some specific reasons for this. The benefits of the clicker include the lack of emotion in the sound, and its consistency. Your clicker will never sound grumpy or tired. But the benefit we are particularly looking for here is the clicker's precision. And we are going to need that precision to mark quite small changes in your dog's behaviour.

Using a clicker is not a long-term commitment. Clickers are mainly used in early training when they double as a release cue. So the click means, 'Yes, I liked it when you sat,' and it also means, 'You can get up now'. The click (or verbal event marker) in our fetch games will be replaced as training progresses by a verbal 'let go' cue that tells the dog to release the toy into your hand.

I understand that some people are not comfortable using a clicker. There was a time when I avoided clickers. To me, they were associated with party tricks and were not a tool for serious dog training. I was wrong; many serious and successful trainers use clickers. And I lacked an understanding of just how powerful a precise event marker can be. While I won't say that you *have* to use a clicker to play these games, I will say that you will disadvantage yourself if you don't. Using a clicker is the best way to communicate with your dog during this process; it is very precise and only temporary. The most important thing you need to know about your event marker, whether you use a word or a click, is that it is a promise. It is your promise to your dog that a reward is on its way – not any old reward but a reward that has a high value to your dog. Remember that high-value rewards reinforce behaviour and that the simplest and most effective reward for all dogs in early training is food.

Arguments against using food

Some people have concerns about using food in dog training. You may have heard that training the retrieve using treats can result in a dog that always spits out the toy at your feet, instead of placing it nicely in your hand. With traditional training this could happen. With shaping, this isn't a problem as we teach the delivery to hand at the beginning of the process rather than the end and because we teach the dog not to let go of the toy until they hear the 'let go' cue. Others are worried that their dog will get fat. This is easily avoided by deducting the food used in training from the dog's daily food allowance and by using healthy and appropriate food as training treats.

Using food in these early games is so important. Much as we would like dogs to play the games for love alone, there is ample evidence that dogs work harder and learn more quickly when reinforced with food than they do when reinforced with praise or a kind word.

Games such as tug can also make good rewards, but they take up a lot of time and in these early games they are not a practical solution as we want to make rapid progress and keep the momentum going. Later on we'll certainly look at other ways of reinforcing your dog, but for now, food is the fastest and most effective way of getting this new training programme under way.

Preparing rewards

Kibble makes a simple basic reward that many dogs value and is easy to handle and hold, but it's important that also you have some higher-value rewards in your toolbox. Leftover chunks of meat from the Sunday joint are perfect training treats. If a roast is not your thing, keep a stock of skin-on chicken breasts in your freezer and cook one up every couple of days or so, for your dog. You can fry, grill or bake them. The reason I recommend leaving the skin on is because the skin and the fat beneath it add a lot of flavour to the meat. You'll need to cut the breast into little chunks and keep these in the refrigerator.

You can feed the dog straight from the refrigerator but for maximum tastiness, let the chicken pieces come to room temperature by taking them out of the fridge about ten minutes before training. Even if your dog is happy to play the games for kibble, it's a great idea to add the occasional real meat treat, just to make things a little more fun. You'll also need those high-value treats when you start to train your dog outdoors, with all the distractions that brings.

If your dog is usually given raw food, then you may also need to buy some kibble or commercial dog treats specifically for training. You can buy treats that are chunks of freeze-dried meat if you really don't want to give kibble to your raw-fed dog.

Treat bags and pots

Rewards need to be delivered promptly to be effective and not interrupt the flow and pace of the games. When you are working indoors, you can often keep your training treats in a pot that is within easy reach. Outdoors you will need a treat bag with a belt that can be worn or attached to your own belt. I like the silicone treat bags with an opening that springs shut rather than you having to unbutton the top or loosen a string; they are also very easy to clean.

Leashes and lines

Towards the end of this course you'll be using a regular clip-on leash in some of the games, and your dog will need to be wearing a strong buckle or clip collar, or a harness, so that you can attach their leash quickly and easily. You may also need a long-line or training leash when you begin outdoor training. A training leash is simply a longer leash with no handle that trails along the ground to be used in an emergency. You can buy training leashes online, or you can improvise with some light rope, but avoid handles as these tend to snag on undergrowth or obstacles on the ground. The long line also needs to clip or be tied on to your dog's harness or collar. I'll be explaining how to use it when we get to stage 5.

Recording your progress

Last, but not least, you'll need a way of charting your progress. It's a good idea to buy a dedicated notebook for this project. I keep a plastic-backed A5 spiral notebook for each dog. If you don't write down what you have done in a training session and life gets in the way for a few days, you'll forget where you got to. Writing down what you achieved and what you want to achieve next time is very motivating and helps you get the next training session off to a flying start.

Training games

Most modern dog training involves a lot of games and some people find this worrying. For them it sounds too much like fun and not enough like training. Game-based training *is* a lot of fun, but happily it is also a very effective way to train a dog. It is simply a way of breaking down training exercises into small achievable chunks.

The training stages

This book is divided into six training stages:

The release

The pick-up

The hold

The delivery and the cues

The wait

The retrieve

Within each of these stages there are five lessons and throughout the first five stages of training, each lesson includes at least one game. The role of that game is to prepare you and your dog for the next lesson. In the final stage of training you will find games that you and your dog will be able to play for the rest of their life.

The games

Each game in this book consists of a series of clearly laid-out steps. You'll play the game several times until you and your dog are ready to move on to the next one. There are detailed instructions for each step and plenty of information to help you know when to start and when to move on. It's a good idea to read through all the steps carefully before you start each game.

I have deliberately made the game steps very detailed and specific, but I don't want you to be tying yourself in knots trying to follow them to the absolute letter, especially if you find that difficult. My aim is to give you a guide for each game and to help you build a solid strategy of increasing the level of difficulty in small increments whenever you work with your dog on a new skill. Think of the steps as a recipe. Your sponge cake would probably be fine if you put in an extra 15g of sugar or flour, but if you changed the proportions of the ingredients too drastically, it might not turn out as you intended. In the same way, if you take three steps when I say two, it probably won't make any difference. But if you change the order of the steps, or change two steps to ten steps, your dog might well fail.

The location

When you first start teaching a dog something new, it is critical that the distractions to the dog are minimal. To minimise distractions, the games in this first section of the book are taught and played indoors. Choose a space or room where it is easy for you to take control. The middle of a busy family area where there are always people milling around is not a good choice. You need to make sure there are no other people or animals in the room. The kitchen, or even the bathroom, can work well. You don't need much space for these games to begin with and you certainly don't need an audience. Put the cat out, and if necessary, hang a 'do not disturb' sign on the door. It should be just you and your dog.

Later on in training, we play the games outside, and it's important that you choose your location wisely and prepare your dog to train there. The important thing to remember is that engagement comes before training. You can't train a dog that has no interest in you and is not paying you any attention. Before you start playing the games in your chosen outdoor location, you need to 'prep' your dog for training. Start by walking about, changing direction frequently and hand feeding treats every few seconds. Is your dog paying attention now? If it is, you can ask your dog to do something simple. It could be a brief sit, or a hand touch. Keep sits or downs very short, feed in position and release the dog after a few seconds. If your dog doesn't know any obedience skills yet, just keep rewarding the dog for following you and for eye contact. Once you have their full attention, you can start to play a game.

Once you have your dog's full attention, you can start to play

Time and frequency

It's a good idea to play twice a day if you can, and to play at least five days a week. If you have to take a break for more than a couple of days, you might need to go back a couple of games rather than starting where you left off.

It doesn't matter what time of day you play but it is important that your dog has not recently eaten a large meal. You want them to be hungry and eager to earn your treats, so play before your dog's mealtimes, not afterwards.

What might happen?

Most chapters have a 'What might happen?' section after the game steps to help you if the game did not go as planned. I don't want you to get the impression that every game is a potential disaster; most of the time, you won't need this section at all as the game will go as planned. The purpose of 'What might happen?' is simply to help you if you get stuck. Reading it through before you play will also help you avoid the most common mistakes. There's also a troubleshooting chapter (see page 211) if you get stuck.

Are you ready?

We're almost ready to begin stage 1. Make sure you have everything you need before starting the game. It's a good idea to keep your toy, clicker and notebook in a convenient place in the room where you'll be playing these first games. Remove any trailing cords or labels from the toy, as these can flap about and be distracting to the dog. Prepare your treats in advance. I always keep a spare box of treats in the freezer so that I never run out. If not using kibble, any fresh treasts should be cut up very small so that the dog can eat one quickly and continue with the game.

There's an introductory chapter that you need to read at each stage, before you start to play the games. Let's head over to that chapter in stage 1 now.

Stage 1:
The release

About the release

This training stage is called 'the release' because the priority in stage 1 is not the dog's ability to interact with the toy, it is the dog's ability to let it go. In each game in this section, one of your goals is to ensure that the dog can physically move away from, and emotionally release, the toy. The closer the dog comes to the toy, the harder it is to 'release' it, so we set your dog up to win by raising the level of difficulty gradually. The final aim for this section is for you to be able to place the toy on the floor, have the dog touch the toy and then disengage from the toy immediately on hearing your release cue. We lead up to this happy moment with five games.

Stage 1: Games

These are the games you'll be teaching your dog in stage 1:

Look at me

Disengage

Not yet

Approach the toy

Touch the toy

It may seem odd that we teach dogs to release an object before they perfect the act of picking something up, but this release of the toy into your care is what keeps the game of fetch going and makes it a team effort. Many dogs will fly through the first three games at the rate of a game per day. But for some dogs, releasing a toy is a difficult thing to do.

Dogs naturally focus on things that they find rewarding. These are the things that they want to eat or possess. It could be food (or the prospect of food), other dogs, a walk or a chance to chase leaves blowing in the wind. Indeed, it could be anything that your dog is motivated to have, watch or do. And it is quite likely to be toys.

Toy crazy?

Many young dogs find toys of any kind extremely exciting. Some of these dogs may have a history of refusing to let go of toys and running off with retrieved items or playing 'keep away'. That's because in the past, these dogs have had far more reinforcement playing with a toy on their own than they have gained by playing in co-operation with a human being. A clue to this as a potential problem is that your dog does not willingly give you toys, even when they bring them to you, and may parade about with them in front of you. And in some cases, the dog can't even take their eyes off a toy when you wave it around in front of them.

Puppies and older dogs that have not been taught to work with humans will assume responsibility for getting what they want. When a dog wants something, such as a treat, they will focus hard on that treat and try to get it for themselves. If they can't reach a treat, or if something is stopping them getting at the treat, they will paw at it or jump at it. You can see why dogs do this – it is a great survival strategy in a wild dog that can expect no help. But your dog has you. And they are about to become very interested in you and everything you do.

Polly finds cuddly toys quite exciting

Teamwork

Retrieving is all about teamwork. To get teamwork going and overcome any toy-crazy tendencies in your dog, you'll be providing some great rewards to reinforce the concept of releasing the toy. Getting the release of the retrieve in place early on in the process also enables you to practise and refine the other parts of the retrieving chain. You won't be able to do this if you have to pursue your dog around the garden and wrestle the toy from their mouth in order to get it back! Once we have the release in place, we can start to add the other components of the retrieve, such the pick-up, the hold and the return.

Letting go

In order to let go of the toy, the dog does, of course, need to have it in their mouth. It's a kind of circular problem but fortunately, there is a neat solution. We can teach the dog to let go of an object 'emotionally' before they make physical contact with the toy. The ability to remove their attention from a toy and focus that attention back on their human partner is something that all dogs can be taught. We mustn't skip this part because if an excitable dog gets a nice squishy toy into its mouth before they have learned to focus on you in the presence of that toy, you will have a problem. It is actually much easier to address that potential problem now, rather than after the dog has started to have fun chucking the toy about in the air, running around with it, or chomping on it and tearing it apart!

Why the release matters so much

Teaching a dog to run hundreds of yards, hunt for an object, and return in style with the prize in their mouth is immensely satisfying. The first time your dog completes a challenging retrieve in public, you'll be overwhelmed with pride. But without the release, you will be left empty-handed. And your joy can easily dissolve into embarrassment. Achieving that release can be surprisingly tricky if you don't establish the principle of releasing the toy right at the very beginning, so it is important to work through these games in order, even if they seem far too simple for your dog.

In the first stage of training, the cue for the dog to 'release' or 'disengage from' the toy will be your event marker. In the first game we use a verbal marker and in the second game I encourage you to switch to a clicker because it will get you where you want to go much faster.

Teaching a dog to fetch is hugely satisfying, but it's also quite involved. You'll need your dog's undivided attention throughout as we seek to eliminate the risk of toy obsession interfering with your training later on, and to build that important connection between your marker and the dog relinquishing the toy. If your dog has little or no interest in toys of any kind, you will be on to the next stage almost immediately.

As you work through the games you will change your dog's understanding of how to get what they want. So that instead of grabbing, snatching or chasing, they'll look to you for help and instructions. Another great reason not to skip this first step is because it builds your dog's ability to pay attention to you and introduces the concept that playing with you is fun.

Game 1:

Look at me

The purpose of this game is to create a shift in your dog's understanding of how to win rewards, by teaching them that looking at your face is a great way to get access to food. If your dog has played focus games before, you'll fly through this one.

Game goals

- The dog looks away from a treat and towards you, in order to win that treat and eat it.
- The dog associates hearing a marker with breaking their focus on the treat.

Game overview

In this game your dog will learn to get what it wants by **giving you what you want**. In this case, what you want is attention, specifically, some eye contact. And you'll give your dog what they want (food) when they give you that eye contact.

The game begins by showing the dog that being around you – and following you – is rewarding. You begin by dropping treats on the floor at intervals. You'll move around while you do this so that your dog starts to follow you and pay attention to you. In the second step, you'll drop a treat on the floor and then wait. Your dog will eventually look up at you to see why the food has stopped. As soon as your dog makes eye contact with you, you'll give your verbal marker, 'yes', and drop another treat.

In the third step, you'll hold a treat out away from your face and reinforce the dog for moving their gaze away from the treat to turn and make eye contact with you. Learning to look away from a treat prepares your dog for learning to look away from other attractive items, including the toy we introduce in the next game. Dogs that have not played this kind of focus game before will generally stare at the treat or try jumping in the air to reach it. They will eventually look at you out of frustration and that is when you give your mark.

Game preparation

You'll need to say your verbal marker clearly and crisply. It needs to be a distinctive and consistent sound to help the dog understand what it means. The word 'yes' in training is a *promise*. It should always be followed by a treat (or other reward).

Shut yourself in a small area indoors with your dog. A kitchen, hall or bathroom is usually ideal. Make sure your dog can't leave and can easily see you as you move around. Remove toys and other distractions from the floor. Make sure family members know not to disturb you until you have finished the session; it will take about five minutes.

You'll need about 30 very small training treats. You can either put them in a pot on a raised surface close to you and out of the dog's reach, in a treat bag clipped to your belt or simply in a pocket.

Game steps

Don't say anything yet, just put 5–6 treats in your hand.

Step 1

Drop a treat on the ground for your dog. Move a couple of steps away and drop another treat. Move around dropping treats at two-second intervals. When you have used up your treats reload your hand and repeat.

Drop a treat every two seconds

Step 2

Drop a treat on the floor to one side of you. Stand still and wait for the dog to look at you. As soon as they do, say 'yes' and drop a treat to the other side. Repeat then reload your hand. Repeat step 2 until the dog looks at you after every treat without you needing to make a noise or attract its attention in any way.

Step 3

Take a treat in your right hand. Let the dog see you have a treat. Stretch your right arm out and wait for the dog to look away from the treat and back at your face. Say 'yes' and throw the treat away from you. Repeat with the other arm.

Hold the treat out and wait for eye contact

Step 4

Sit on a chair or on the floor and repeat steps 2 and 3.

What might happen?

Often the dog will look at your face very briefly, then look back at the treat again. That brief head turn can be tricky to spot, so you need to watch the dog very closely and say 'yes' the second they make that glance. It doesn't matter if the dog looks away after your marker, you still need to follow it up with a treat. Don't worry if you sometimes miss one or two glances. The dog will look again and you will get another chance.

When to move on

Play this game until your dog is repeatedly focusing on your face to get treats and not focusing on the treats in your hand. If your dog is an old hand at eye contact, you'll be able to run through this game once and move straight on to the next one. With most dogs you'll need to play two or three times, then it's on to the next game.

Game 2:
Disengage

In the first game we taught the dog to turn away from food and look at your face in order to get access to reinforcement. In game 2, the distraction is the retrieve toy. Dogs vary widely in their attitude towards toys. Some dogs won't be interested in the retrieve toy at this point. This isn't a problem, and if it applies to your dog, you'll fly through this lesson very quickly. Other dogs get very excited around toys and will need practice before they can quickly disengage from the toy.

Game goals

- The dog looks away from a toy and back towards you in order to win a treat and eat it.
- The dog associates hearing a marker with breaking their focus on the toy.

Game overview

This game helps the dog to understand that trying to get the toy for themselves is not productive, whereas relinquishing the toy leads to a tasty reward. You'll be presenting the toy to your dog at intervals, while holding the toy out of the dog's reach. Each time you present the toy you want the dog to look away from it and offer you eye contact. You'll mark this eye contact and remove the toy from your dog's view while you reward the dog with a treat. Removing the toy from view sets the dog up to look at the toy again when you bring it out of hiding.

Game preparation

Remember to choose an area where you won't be disturbed and where your dog won't be distracted for this and all future games. You'll need your clicker and treats to hand.

Presenting the toy means making it visible for the dog to look at. You'll need to decide how you are going to hide the toy in between each presentation. You can hold it behind your back, tuck it under your arm, or place it on a table. Think about how you are going to keep the toy out of your dog's reach. If you have a big dog this may mean standing up to play the game. With small dogs, it's often best to sit on a chair. Practise presenting the toy *without your dog present* until you feel comfortable doing it.

Game steps

Step 1

With the toy in your hand, stretch your arm out to the side. Keep the toy still while the dog looks at it and wait for the dog to look back at your face.

Step 2

As soon as the dog looks at you – click. Immediately after the click throw the dog a tasty treat. Put the toy behind your back or out of the dog's sight as you do so. Repeat twice more.

Step 3

Switch hands so the toy is in your other hand and repeat from step 1 with the other arm.

Top Polly looks at the toy
Above Polly switches her attention to me

Moving on

In the next game we'll be increasing the power of the toy as a distraction, by placing it on the floor. You are ready to move on as soon as the dog can look away from the toy in your hand and back at your face, every time you present it.

Game 3:

Not yet!

Having taught the dog to disengage from the toy in your hand, you'll now make sure that the dog can do the same with the toy on the floor. This is a quick lesson; you'll probably only need to play this game once. The name of this game is 'Not yet!' because you are not quite at the point where you want your dog to interact with the toy. But you are making the toy much more interesting and distracting by placing it on the floor.

Game goal

- The dog gives you eye contact while the toy is on the floor.

Game overview

The purpose of 'Not yet' is to ensure that your dog is able to focus on you even when a toy is within reach. You'll be placing a toy on the floor and reinforcing the dog for ignoring or moving their gaze away from that toy to give you some eye contact. For some dogs, having the toy at ground level makes the toy a lot more interesting and attractive. You'll need to be careful to make sure that your dog can't grab the toy and run off with it! Sitting on a chair with the toy by your foot gives you that little bit of extra control.

To get to this point, you will start by holding the toy out to the side just as you did in the previous lesson. In the second step, you'll hold the toy much lower and in the third step, you'll place it on the ground. You don't need to wiggle the toy this time or do anything to encourage the dog to look at it. All you want from your dog is some eye contact.

Once the toy is on the floor you don't need to keep picking it up again, you'll leave it on the floor for the rest of the game. You'll move the dog away from you and the toy by throwing treats and they'll keep coming back again to earn the next click.

Game preparation

Start the game by sitting on a chair so that you can easily reach down and place the toy on the floor. You'll place the toy next to your foot, so that you can step on the toy if the dog should decide to make a grab for it. You'll be throwing treats out in front of you so that your dog has to run away from you to get them and then run back towards you to earn the next click.

Game steps

Before each step throw a treat way out in front of you to move your dog away from you.

Step 1

Hold the toy out to one side, just as you did in the previous lesson. Click when your dog makes eye contact, remove the toy, then throw a treat away from you. Repeat twice more.

Step 2

Hold the toy out to one side, much lower and close to the ground. Click as soon as you get eye contact, remove the toy and throw the treat away from you. Repeat, touching one end of the toy to the floor.

Step 3

Place the toy on the floor in front of you. Be ready to click as the dog turns back to look at you and throw another treat behind the dog. Don't wait for the dog to reach you.

Repeat five times. And pick the toy up as the dog collects the final treat.

Keep the toy near your foot so that you can step on it if the dog attempts to pick it up

What might happen?

Don't worry if the dog doesn't even acknowledge the presence of the toy. We'll be teaching them to interact with the toy in future lessons.

If the dog **doesn't go after the treat** when you click and continues towards the toy put your foot on the toy so that the dog cannot pick it up. Press a juicy treat right up against the dog's nose. When the dog has eaten the treat, throw another juicy treat well away from the toy and pick up the toy. Play the game from step 1 again, until the dog can break away from the toy on the floor **every time** on hearing the click.

Moving on

There's no need to linger on this game. Just make sure you can place the toy on the floor without the dog making a grab for it, and that the dog is able to give you eye contact while the toy is on the floor. Reward your dog a few times for this eye contact and move on to the next game.

Game 4:

The approach

Now that we know that your dog is able to ignore the toy on the floor, we are going to shift our focus back to the toy again. We'll stop reinforcing the dog for eye contact and start reinforcing them for interacting with the toy. We'll use our click to mark those interactions.

The click has two roles now. It continues to mark the events we want to reinforce, but it also acts as a release cue. That means that the click signals the end of the behaviour we are reinforcing and your dog must respond to this release cue by breaking away from the toy.

Game goals

- The dog approaches the toy.
- The dog breaks off their approach and refocuses their attention on you when they hear your click.
- Breaking off the interaction with the toy is our top priority. If you allow the dog to pick up the toy at this point, you may find that they won't let go on hearing your click.

Game overview

You'll place the toy on the floor and imagine a circle around it. The dog needs to enter this circle. And when they do, you will click. The reason that the dogs breaks away from the toy on hearing the click is that the previous three lessons have taught the dog that paying attention to you when you click is very rewarding. So breaking off their approach towards the toy is a natural reaction to hearing the click.

To begin with you and the toy will be in the same circle so the dog automatically gets a reward as they come back towards you in search of more treats. In step 2 you will move outside the circle so that the dog has to purposefully approach the toy in order to earn a treat. You'll vary the direction in which you throw your treats, so the dog is clear that it is **approaching the toy** that makes the click happen, not the fact that they just walked past your kitchen table.

The toy will be on the floor during this game and many of the games that follow. When you want to end the game, or if you need to interrupt the game for any reason, throw a treat away from the toy and pick the toy up. It's better if the dog doesn't see you pick it up, and they must not be able to interact with the toy while you are not engaged with them.

Game preparation

You'll need your toy and a pot of treats and a quiet place to play.

Game steps

Step 1: Stand in the circle

Throw a treat away from you and place the toy on the floor near your foot, while the dog is collecting the treat. Imagine a circle just over 1 m in diameter around the toy. Click as soon as the dog moves into the circle. Repeat several times.

Step 2: Move out of the circle

Throw a treat away from you and step outside the circle. Click as soon as the dog moves into the circle. Repeat several times moving in different directions around the toy.

Step 3: Shrink the circle

Repeat step 2 but shrink your imaginary circle to about 50cm in diameter. Repeat several times.

When you play the game again, you can ignore steps 1 and 2 and play step 3 only.

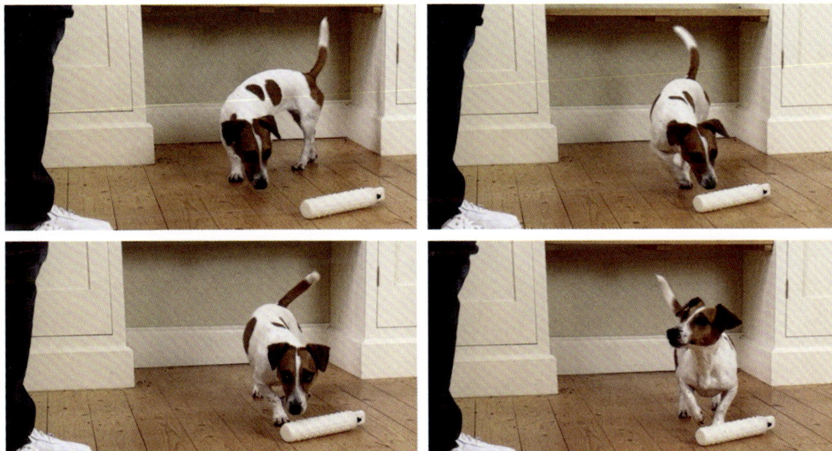

Top row left You are looking for a purposeful approach
Top row right Click just before the dog touches the toy
Above row left The dog should acknowledge the click
Above row right And breakaway from the toy to refocus on you

Keep moving around the room so the dog approaches the toy from different directions

What might happen?

The most common problem in this game is that your dog gets too close to the toy. They might pounce on it, knock it around or even pick it up. There are two likely causes of the dog getting too close. Either you clicked too late or your dog ignored the click. You can fix the former by clicking the moment the dog turns towards the toy after collecting their treat. You may need to throw the treat further away from the toy to achieve this. If your dog ignores the click, put your foot on the toy so they cannot pick it up, and press the treat to the end of the dog's nose until they eat it. Then pick up the toy and play the previous game for a couple more sessions before coming back to this one.

Moving on

When the dog is purposefully approaching the toy and breaking away from the toy on hearing the click, then you can move on to the next game.

Game 5:

The touch

In the last lesson we focused our efforts on ensuring that your dog will approach and acknowledge the retrieve toy but will turn away from it immediately on hearing a click. This will help ensure that the dog is always able to release the toy **on your cue**, rather than wanting to run off with it or play with it. Now it's time to move the goalposts a little and ask your dog to make contact with the toy.

Game goal

- The dog touches the toy with their mouth or nose.

Game overview

Each time we move our training goalposts, we stop reinforcing the behaviour that we've captured so far and wait for the dog to give us something better. In this case we want them to go closer to the toy. You'll start where you finished the previous game, by reinforcing the dog for entering an imaginary circle and making visual contact with the toy. Then we'll move the goalposts by shrinking that circle to just a few centimetres, and finally you'll wait for the dog to actually touch the toy with their nose or muzzle. You'll throw treats away from the toy to reset the dog.

Game preparation

You may find it helpful to sit down for this game so that you can observe the dog more closely.

Game steps

Click and throw a treat to move the dog away from you and place the toy on the floor.

Step 1: Click early

Click and treat the dog for approaching the toy. Click early, before the dog is within half a metre of the toy. Repeat several times.

Step 2: Almost touch

Click and treat the dog when their nose is within 5cm or so of the toy. Don't wait for the actual touch, try to click the *intention* to touch. Repeat several times.

Step 3: Touch

Wait for the dog to **make contact with the toy** with their nose or mouth. Click and throw a treat as soon as the dog touches the toy. Repeat several times.

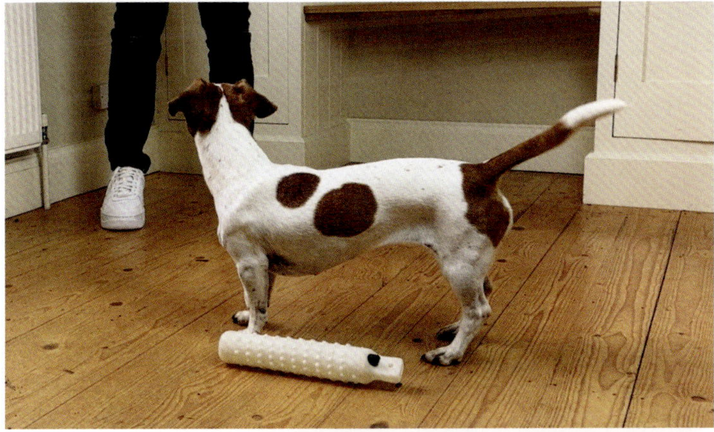

Throw the treats so that the dog has to approach the toy from different directions

What might happen?

Occasionally a dog will grab on to the toy on that first approach and will not release it on your click. If this happens, press a really juicy treat right up against your dog's nose until they release the toy. Then go back to clicking just the early part of the approach and more thoroughly reinforcing disengagement from the toy for another day or two.

Sometimes interaction with the toy may happen quite quickly; sometimes it's not the interaction we want! For example, sometimes, the dog will knock the toy so hard it rolls under a chair or gets stuck in a corner. You can reposition it with your foot if necessary while your dog is collecting their treat. It's important not to accidentally teach the dog to use their paws to make contact with the dummy, as those paws won't help us when it comes to lifting the toy off the ground. In this game, no clicks are given for paw contact.

If at first your dog isn't interested in touching the toy, it's a matter of waiting and making your circle ever smaller, until the dog makes that first touch. Sometimes you will have to move your goalposts by only a few centimetres at a time in order to keep the rate of reinforcement high. Watch your dog closely so you don't miss that first touch. It takes practice to get the timing right here, so don't worry if you accidentally click after the dog has turned away. Just make sure you click very early for the next two or three approaches, to avoid reinforcing that turn away.

If you have any of the problems above, you may be training in too large a space or with too many distractions for your dog. Switch your location to somewhere more boring, such as the bathroom, small hallway or even a puppy playpen.

Moving on

When your dog will repeatedly approach and touch the toy and immediately break away on hearing the click, you have completed stage 1 of this course. This is an awesome achievement so give yourself a treat too. And then it's time to move up a gear and on to the next stage when you'll get your dog picking up the toy.

Stage 2:
The pick-up

About the pick-up

Welcome to the second stage of fetch training! You've made a great start. You already have a dog that will purposefully touch the fetch toy when it is placed on the ground, and that will disengage from that toy on hearing the click. Next, we need to get your dog to pick the toy up. Going from touching an item to picking it up is a huge leap for some dogs, so you will be breaking it down into achievable steps.

Stage 2: Games

These are the games you'll be teaching your dog in stage 2:

Away

Open wide

Lift

Airborne

Go pick up

In game 6 you'll get your dog moving away from you to consolidate their understanding of the importance of touching the toy. In game 7 you'll bring the toy back in close where you can see what's happening and start reinforcing open-mouth touches. Then you'll progress to reinforcing the dog for biting or grasping at the toy with more purpose.

This process requires you to watch your dog's mouth very closely, and you may find it easier to do this at your dog's level. It depends a bit on how your dog behaves. If they are able to focus on the toy and carry on with the game while you sit on the floor, then do that. But if they find you too distracting when you join them on the floor you may need to sit in a low chair so that you can see what their mouth is doing. It isn't always easy to judge whether or not the dog is opening their mouth, especially if they are very quick, so don't worry if you make a few mistakes – clicker training is very forgiving.

In game 8, after you have made some progress with the open mouth, you will switch your focus from the dog's jaws to the toy itself. You'll be watching the toy very closely and marking the moment that any part of it lifts up off the ground. This stage in training can be tricky; Polly was stuck here for a while and that is common. Don't worry, I have lots of ways to help you and your dog succeed!

Sometimes the opposite happens, and you can get quick wins at this stage. The dog may rush out and actually pick the toy right up before you get the chance to click for an open mouth. This is great, but be careful, there is potential here for ignoring the release cue. It's very tempting to applaud the dog when it grabs the toy and lifts it up and then admire them carrying the toy around. After all, this is what you've been waiting for, isn't it? But it's important that you DON'T do this. Click as soon as **any part** of the toy leaves the ground and remember that the dog **must let go of the toy** on hearing the click. If you are having problems with this, turn to the troubleshooting chapter on page 211.

By the end of stage 2, possibly just a few days from now, your dog will be picking up the toy.

Polly and I decided to switch to this red bone during stage 2

Game 6:

Away

In game 5 you taught your dog to repeatedly touch a toy that you placed on the floor by your feet. The chances are that your dog is quite casual about this nose contact and you may find it's not always easy to tell if they have accidentally knocked the toy or if their actions are more deliberate. What we are going to do today, is make sure that your dog's interaction with the toy is purposeful. We'll ensure that the dog is making an active decision to both approach and then touch the toy, rather than bumping it about in an accidental way.

Game goal

- The dog moves away from you to touch a toy several feet away, returns to you for a treat, then goes back to the toy for another touch.

Game overview

In this game you are going to feed the dog from your hand instead of throwing the treat. The dog then has to make the decision to move away from you, the source of food, towards the toy to make a touch, then return to you in order to get their reward (rather than wait for you to throw something). This helps to make the dog's actions more deliberate and deepens their understanding of the importance of the toy. And of the importance of repeatedly checking in with you.

It's important that we maintain the dog's ability to abandon interaction with the toy when they hear the click. The way to ensure this is to start by clicking the dog as they move towards the toy, preferably before they reach it, let alone touch it. Starting with an early click, if possible, helps to consolidate the dog's understanding that the release cue **overrides** their desire to interact with the toy.

You'll start very close to the toy. Once the dog has made a couple of touches, you'll build the distance from the toy gradually, by stepping away from it before you feed the treat. Each time the dog returns to the toy, they have to travel a bit further. When you come to the end of each game, you'll throw a treat well away from the dog and pick up the toy while they are collecting their treat.

Game preparation

Moving towards a toy before touching raises the excitement level a bit. Some dogs will rush to the toy at speed, and it will be harder for them to spin around on your click than for a dog that ambles towards the toy, so make sure you have some very juicy treats for this game. Roast meat or cheese can work well. Give one to the dog just before you start so that they know what they will be getting when they break away from that toy.

You'll be standing up for this game, so you'll need a treat bag or pocket, or a handy surface to work alongside where you can place your treat pot. Load your hand with treats before you start.

Game steps

Throw a treat behind you before you start. While the dog is collecting it, place the toy on the ground in front of you and take a small step back.

Step 1: Click the intention to touch

Click as the dog moves towards the toy. Try to click just **before they touch it**. When the dog returns to you, feed it a treat from your hand. Now take another small step back as the dog travels out to the toy (you are now two paces away from the toy). Repeat once more, finishing three paces from the toy.

Step 2: Click the touch

Move close to the toy and repeat step 1 but this time the dog must actually touch the toy to earn the click. Step back a pace each time the dog travels to the toy, then stand still and feed it from your hand when the dog returns to you. If you have space build up to five or six paces between you and the toy.

To end the game, when the dog returns after the final touch, throw a treat well away from the toy and then pick the toy up.

Travelling away from you to touch the toy helps build awareness that the toy is important

What might happen?

Sometimes the distance that the dog is having to travel between you and the toy can be a distraction for the dog. This is especially true for calmer, quieter dogs that are not in too much of a hurry. At four or five steps they may start to hesitate over going out to touch the toy or may offer you other behaviours such as a sit, or a jump up. These dogs may need you to patiently build up to five or six steps more gradually over two or three sessions. If your dog hesitates or slows down as the distance increases, move closer to the toy again. Practise a few times close to the toy and increase the distance again more slowly, taking smaller steps or by stepping back every second or third treat.

Moving on

Play this game in at least two different sessions. When your dog is comfortable travelling back and forth to touch the toy, then collect a treat, then touch the toy again, it's time to start teaching your dog to take hold of that toy in their mouth. If in doubt, play this game a few more times; there's no hurry.

Game 7:

Open wide

This is where the magic of shaping really gets going. We'll get the dog touching the toy, then we'll move the goalposts and ask for an open-mouth touch. When we move the goalposts while shaping new behaviours, it's important that we don't allow the dog to experience failure too often. As far as the dog is concerned, no click and treat equals failure. So, if your dog has poked the toy maybe ten or so times without reinforcement, you will see a rapid drop off in the number of attempts. The dog may even give up and wander off to find something better to do. If you have three or four failed attempts in a row, go back and practise a behaviour your dog can win, before trying again. This helps to keep them in the game.

We'll start with a few easy wins for the dog, then we'll withhold the rewards and wait for the dog to try out some different ways to interact with the toy. At any point during this game or the next one, your dog may suddenly pick the toy up. It's an exciting moment but remember that you still need to ensure that the click is always followed by the release! If you do get a quick win, click and treat as soon as the toy leaves the ground. Don't jeopardise your release by waiting for the dog to start moving with the toy.

Game goal

- Our goal for this lesson is simple: open-mouth contact with the toy.

Game overview

Step 1 reinforces a simple touch. After a few repetitions you'll move to step 2 where you stop rewarding touches and wait for an open mouth. Usually the dog will poke and push the toy a few times but after a few attempts they'll have a quick nibble, usually at one end. You are waiting to get a glimpse of some teeth! Be ready for this and click.

You may find that the dog paws at the toy to begin with. You'll ignore this and wait for them to interact with the toy using their mouth. They don't have to lift the toy, just touch it with a partly open mouth. After each click, you'll throw the treat well away from you to reset the dog so that they can return for another try. When you come to the end of each game, throw a treat well away from the dog and pick up the toy while they are collecting their reward.

Game preparation

In this game you won't be moving around, you'll stay close to the toy so that you can see what's going on. If you can sit on the floor without the dog getting excited, you may find it easier to see what their mouth is doing that way. Otherwise sit on a low chair and focus on watching your dog's jaws.

Game steps

Throw a treat to move the dog away from you.

Step 1: Click any mouth touch

Put the toy on the floor in front of you. Click as soon as the dog touches it. Throw the treat away from you. Repeat two or three times.

Step 2: Click open-mouth touch

Wait for the dog to place their open mouth on the toy. You may need to bend or lean to see what's happening. Click for any open-mouth contact with the toy, then throw the treat away from you. Repeat 5–10 times, then stop the game and play again later. Once you are getting open-mouth touches repeatedly, drop step 1.

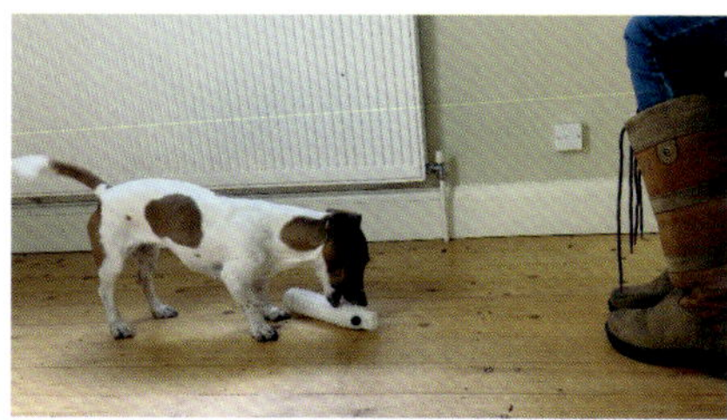

Sitting on a chair or on the floor will give you a better view of the dog's mouth

What might happen?

The most likely problem at this point is that the dog simply doesn't open their mouth. They may try pushing the toy with their paws, or they may try bumping it harder and harder with their nose.

Ignore any contact with paws, reinforcing paw touches won't help you. But if there is no sign of an open mouth after a few bumps it's important to keep the rate of reward high. In this case, you can reinforce harder nose touches, or double nose touches for a while then make a second attempt at capturing an open mouth. Be patient; sooner or later the dog will open their mouth. And once you have that first open-mouth contact, more will follow.

Moving on

When you are getting eight or nine open-mouth touches out of every ten contacts that the dog makes with the toy, it's time to move on to the next game. Let's start to get that toy up off the ground!

Game 8: Lift

This game is an interim step to bridge the gap between mouthing at the toy and actually picking it up. Don't worry if this process feels a little slow. This can be a very quick step for some dogs; with others it can take a few sessions for the dog to figure it out. I'll explain what to do.

Game goal

- The dog lifts one end of the toy clear of the ground.

Game overview

In this game you are going to shift your focus to the toy. You are not going to worry about what the dog is doing with their mouth, instead you will focus on marking the moment that any part of the toy lifts off the floor. You are not going to ask for much, just 1–2cm will do. The lift may be very brief indeed to start with.

You'll throw a reset treat at the beginning of the game to move the dog away from you and while the dog is collecting it, you'll put the toy on the floor in front of you.

Game preparation

You'll need your toy, treats and clicker. As in the previous game, the dog may move the toy around a bit, so avoid placing the toy too close to objects or walls, and be ready to reposition it if necessary. It will help if you are close to the toy. Get down on the ground if you can or sit on a low chair. You may get lucky and reach full lift-off in this lesson. But that's not our goal. When it comes to spotting the first lift, you'll need to keep looking very closely at the toy and be quick with your clicker.

Game steps

Drop a treat to move the dog away from you.

Step 1: Open-mouth touch

Place the toy close to you, on the floor. Click as soon as the dog touches the toy with an open mouth. Throw the treat away from you. Repeat twice more.

Step 2: Partial lift

Wait for either end of the toy to lift up in the air. You may need to bend or lean to see what's happening! Click as soon as you see any part of the toy leave the ground. Throw a treat away from you. Repeat until you have captured 5–6 of these partial lifts. Then stop the game and play again later.

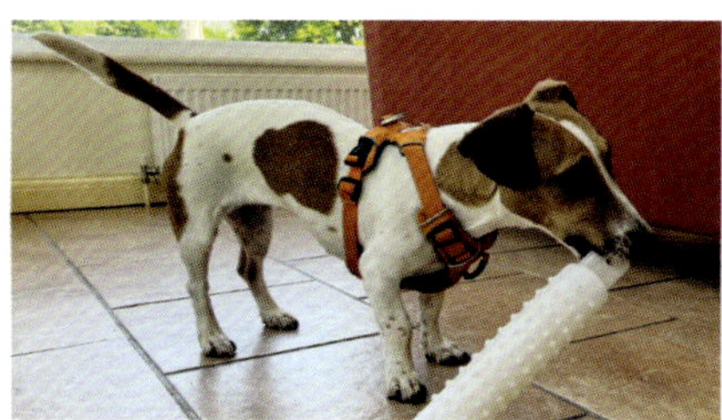

It took Polly several sessions to get to this point

What might happen?

Just as in the previous game, it's important that we don't allow the dog to fail too many times. If the toy is not being lifted at all after being touched by the dog five or six times, don't let the dog keep failing. Instead, start to click for more intense mouthing of the toy, a wider mouth or a firmer grasp of the toy. Then try holding out for a lift again in your next session. Make sure you keep the games short and successful. Play three or four times a day for a couple of days, and if you are still struggling after playing half a dozen times, turn to the troubleshooting chapter on page 211, so that I can help you get back on track.

Moving on

Don't panic if you don't get a lift in the first session or two. This is a common sticking point – Polly and I were stuck here for a while, and you'll get past it as we did.

When part of the toy is lifting off the floor repeatedly, and when this has happened in two consecutive sessions, it's time to move on to the next game.

Game 9:
Airborne

You now have a dog that will lift one end of your chosen retrieving toy off the ground and then disengage on your click. That's a huge achievement! In this lesson you are going to focus on getting a full lift. You want to see the **whole toy** clear the ground. It doesn't have to be by much, a couple of centimetres will do.

Game goal

- The dog lifts the toy clear of the ground and drops it when you click.

Game overview

You'll start where you left off in the previous lesson. You'll throw a reset treat, place the toy on the floor and click when one end of that toy leaves the ground. After a few repetitions, you'll stop rewarding the dog for that partial lift. You'll set a new standard – the toy must leave the ground completely. As always, when we move the goalposts, the dog may try out some behaviours that you don't want, such as pawing or pushing the toy instead. You'll ignore these and wait for a lift. You'll also start feeding the dog from your hand now as this prepares the dog for always returning to your hand as part of the retrieving process.

It's better to click early than late. Do NOT wait to see if the dog will hold on to the toy, click **the moment** the toy clears the ground.

Game preparation

Sit on a chair or the floor so that you can clearly see what's happening with the toy.

Game steps

To start the game, throw a treat away from you and place the toy on the floor in front of you.

Step 1: Partial lift

Wait for the dog to grasp the toy and lift either end clear of the ground. You may need to bend or lean to see what's happening. Click and treat as soon as you see any part of the toy leave the ground. Repeat a couple of times.

Step 2: Airborne

Click as soon as the toy is clear of the floor (not touching the floor at all). Feed the dog a treat. Click and treat the dog two or three times for lifting the toy clear of the floor.

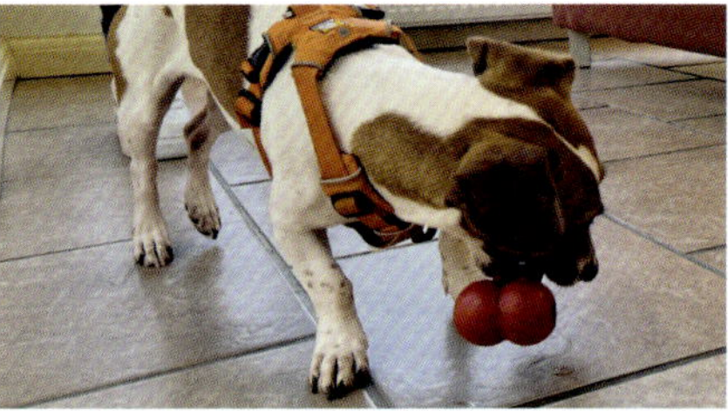

Left Here's Bonnie showing you the point at which you need to click
Right The first full lift is a great moment!

What might happen?

We don't want the dog to lose interest in the game through lack of reinforcement. If the dog makes five or more attempts at lifting the toy and only lifts one end each time, go back to clicking partial lifts for the rest of this session and play from the beginning again in the next session. Next time you play, try to reinforce only more vigorous partial lifts, so that one end of the toy is coming higher off the ground as the game progresses.

Occasionally, this game can drag on for many sessions. If you feel progress has ground to a halt after several more sessions, or you are getting disheartened, turn to the troubleshooting chapter on page 211. Polly got stuck at this point for over two weeks and I made the decision to switch toys, which is one of several options you'll find explained in that section.

Moving on

Count each time your dog makes contact with the toy as one 'attempt' and a full lift as a successful attempt. Nine out of ten successful attempts in a single session is a good rate to aim for. Once you've achieved that, it's time to move on to the final game in this section.

Game 10:

Go pick up

Well done! Your toy is finally airborne; you and your dog have completed some fantastic teamwork. It's now time to combine that momentary 'pick-up' you have achieved with the 'away' game we played at the beginning of this section. This establishes a pattern of the dog moving away from you to the toy and back again for a treat. Leaving and returning, in a continuous loop until you end the game, is at the heart of a game of fetch. So, even though the dog isn't carrying the toy back at this point, you are building an important behaviour pattern.

Game goal

- The dog picks up the toy and **drops it on hearing your clic**k. The dog then comes to you for their treat before returning to pick up the toy again.

Game overview

You'll be asking the dog to move away from you to reach the toy, lift the toy up off the ground and drop it immediately on hearing your click. This game is played with you standing up because you are going to be stepping backwards from the toy. You'll start with the toy at your feet and as the game progresses you'll gradually move away from it. Some dogs are not comfortable with picking up a toy at some distance from you, so we need to build up those distances in very small increments.

Game preparation

You'll need to give yourself as much room to back away as you can. A hallway can be ideal, but if you need to use a different room, remember to play the previous game in that area a couple of times first, so that the dog is comfortable there. As you'll be on the move, you'll need to have a treat bag attached to your waist or pocket.

Game steps

Throw a reset treat and put the toy on the floor in front of you.

Put the toy out while the dog is collecting a treat from behind you

Step 1

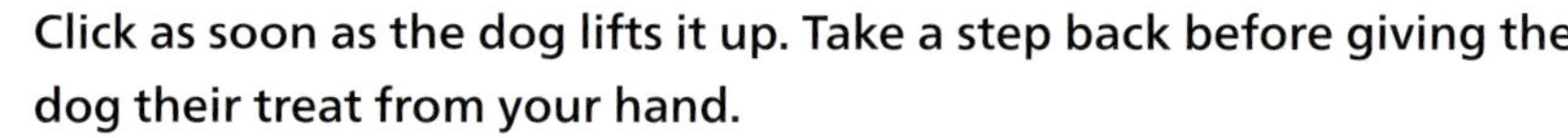

Click as soon as the dog lifts it up. Take a step back before giving the dog their treat from your hand.

Step 2

Wait for the dog to lift the toy again. Click and take two steps back before delivering the treat.

Step 3

Wait for the dog to lift the toy again. Click and take three steps back before delivering the treat.

Step 4

If there is space in your training area, repeat at four and five steps.

When the dog returns after the final lift, throw a treat well away from the toy and pick the toy up. You can repeat the game from the beginning a couple of times in a session if you want to.

What might happen?

Sometimes you'll get a dog that returns to partial lifting at this point, possibly picking the toy up by one end and dragging it along. If this happens, it's important to go back to game 9 and focus on clicking for nice clean high lifts for a couple of sessions.

Moving on

You don't need to spend too much time on this game. Once your dog is happy to leave your side after each treat and return to the toy over a distance of four or five steps, it is time to move on to the next stage in training.

Stage 3:
The hold

About the hold

For the next few games we are going to work on your dog's ability to hold a toy in their mouth until you tell them to let go. Having a dog hold on to a retrieve until you are ready to take it from them is an important part of the retrieving chain. For some dogs, the hold is the trickiest part of the retrieve and this section is likely to take a little longer to complete than the previous one. It's worth persisting because a reliable hold is a great skill for any dog to learn and, fortunately, there are several ways to achieve a hold. We'll be using at least two methods in the games to come. Below are the three main ways that I teach the hold and I'll explain how to choose the right method for your dog depending on their progress.

The natural hold

The following hold

The catch and click hold

The natural hold

If the dog has a natural tendency to hold the toy after picking it up, the natural hold is a quick and easy way to teach a dog to hold a toy. It's simply a question of reinforcing this tendency and lengthening the duration of the hold in achievable increments of a second or two. This tendency to hold on to objects is common in retrievers and spaniels, as well as many other dogs.

The following hold

A lot of dogs enjoy running around with a toy, even if they spit it out as soon as they come to a standstill. This method utilises the dog's natural tendency to hang on to a toy while they are moving. With this method you increase the duration of the hold by backing away from the dog as they return to you after the pick-up. It can be difficult to transition from a moving to a stationary hold, because of the dog's tendency to spit out the toy as soon as they stop moving, but the transition is relatively easy for many dogs.

The catch and click hold

This third method works involves going back to the pick-up with the dog at your feet and putting your hand under the dog's mouth to catch the toy as they release on your click. After catching for a while you can start to delay the appearance of your hand until the dog drops the toy and it lands on the floor. When this happens, the dog gets no reward. Over time, the dog figures out that in this game, the toy has to land in your hand in order for them to earn a click and a treat. Catch and click can take a little longer than the first two methods, which is why we often try those first, but it's a reliable method.

Which method?

Building on the duration of a dog's natural tendency to hold on to the toy is the simplest approach. The downside of the natural hold as a method is that many dogs simply don't have that tendency. They are what I call 'spitters'. They grab the toy and spit it out almost immediately. It is possible to get a hold in a dog like this by reinforcing the tiniest increase in hold duration – I'm talking about milliseconds here. There's more detail in the troubleshooting chapter (see page 211), but building duration can be a frustrating way to start if your dog happens to be a 'spitter'.

For that reason, the method we are going to begin with, is the following hold. We'll start by getting your dog to take a single step with the toy in their mouth and go from there. It's quite likely that your dog has done this already, in which case you'll be off to a flying start.

Game 11:
Lift and follow

You now have a dog that will move away from you to pick up a toy and drop that toy when you give your release cue. Today we are going to show the dog that the pick-up is just the beginning, we can have a lot more fun with this toy than simply picking it up and dropping it again! The object of this game is to get your dog moving with the toy in their mouth.

Game goal

- The dog goes out to the toy, picks it up and takes three steps towards you with the toy in their mouth.

Game overview

Your role is to capture the dog in the act of moving towards you while holding the toy. To trigger that movement, you'll be stepping backwards to encourage the dog to follow you. You'll start to move backwards *before you mark*. The dog wants to move towards you because you are where treats happen. Some dogs want the toy too; others just forget to let go. Either way, they take a step *with the toy in their mouth*. That's what you are waiting for, that one step. You'll mark it, they'll spit out the toy on your mark, and you'll give the dog a treat at your side.

Sounds great, doesn't it? Only with some dogs, this doesn't happen. The second they see you move, they drop the toy and run towards you. These dogs care more about you departing with their treats than they care about the toy. If the dog doesn't take that step, but drops the toy instead, you'll stand still and wait for them to pick up the toy again. This time you won't take a step back but will click as soon as they lift the toy off the ground. And you'll go back to doing this a few times, then try backing away again. The lift and follow behaviour we are looking for will usually happen within two or three sessions of playing the game. And I will explain on page 96 what to do if it doesn't. The number of steps that the dog takes at each stage of the game is not set in stone. They are guidelines to keep you on track with adding more movement in tiny increments. You don't need to worry if the dog fits in more steps than outlined in the instructions before you click.

Game preparation

Make sure there is plenty of space behind you so that you can step back without bumping into anything.

Game steps

To start the game, throw a treat behind you and place the toy on the floor in front of you.

Click while the dog is moving towards you

Step 1

Do not click as the dog lifts the toy, instead start to slowly walk backwards. Click as soon as the dog takes a single step in your direction with the toy in their mouth. Feed the dog when they reach you. **In your first session,** repeat 8–10 times and **stop the game at this point.** In future sessions repeat three times.

Vary the direction, just one step is all you need to get started

Step 2

As the dog lifts the toy and turns towards you, start to walk backwards. Click as soon as the dog takes two steps in your direction with the toy in their mouth. Feed the dog when they reach you. Repeat twice more.

Step 3

As the dog lifts the toy and turns towards you start to step back. Click as soon as the dog takes three steps in your direction with the toy in their mouth. Feed the dog when they reach you. Repeat once more.

What might happen?

You may find that the dog reaches you before you click and drops the toy at your feet. That's okay. Just take a couple more steps back before feeding them the treat to put some distance between the dog and the toy before their next attempt. And try to walk back a little faster next time!

What if the dog drops the toy before you click?

The dog knows that they will not get a treat unless they hear the click, so if the dog releases the toy before you click, just wait for the dog to pick up the toy again. Don't click until the toy is off the ground. And don't keep attempting step 2 again and again if you are not succeeding. At this stage, without plenty of reinforcement, the dog will probably lose their enthusiasm for picking up the toy quite quickly. Instead, go back and repeat step 1 a few more times before trying step 2 again.

You can't count the steps

Some dogs like to play this game at a run and are so quick that it's difficult to count those steps. In this case, you can use seconds instead. Start by trying for a one-second hold. Just count 'one thousand' in your head as you step back then click (provided the dog still has the toy in their mouth).

The dog gets excited after lifting the toy

This game is quite exciting for some dogs. You may find your dog gets quite playful, maybe pouncing on the toy (and sending it flying) or moving away from you before dropping it again. If this happens wait patiently for the dog to pick the toy up again and click the instant they lift the toy off the ground. In effect you return to step 1 for a couple of reps, then try again at step 2.

The dog is not lifting very high

Some dogs may start to drag rather than carry the toy at this point, often just holding one end. If you let them just drop the toy, they'll often pick it up again with a better hold. My young lab Bonnie did this a few times. If your dog is dragging the toy on more than one or two occasions, it's a good idea to spend a couple of sessions where you just click for higher lifts.

You find it difficult to remember what you are meant to be doing

Walking backwards, remembering to click, counting the dog's steps, there is a lot to remember in this game. Don't worry, it will all fall into place as you practise. And really, it doesn't matter if you don't get the step counts exactly right provided the duration of your moving hold is increasing.

You keep clicking at the same time as the dog lets go

The most frustrating mistake is when you click at exactly the same time as the dog spits out the toy, thus reinforcing the spit. If this happens, then on the next repetition I want you to deliberately wait until the dog drops the toy. Just keep walking until they let go. Keep your thumb off the clicker! Do this a couple of times then follow it immediately with a couple of reps where you click as soon as the toy lifts off the ground. Don't wait for a follow, just watch for the lift and then click that. This experience illustrates for the dog the difference between letting go before the click (no reward) and dropping when they hear the click (reward).

You'll probably find it exciting to see the dog moving towards you with the toy in their mouth and the temptation to delay that click and get a few more steps in is great! But, if you push this too far you risk having the dog spit the toy before the click, so resist the urge to increase those steps too quickly.

Moving on

Play the this game over the next few days – two or three times a day is ideal, each time repeating the same process. Make a note of what happened each time. When you succeed in completing step 3 on two separate occasions, you are ready to move on to game 12. If, after playing the game at least five times over at least two days you *haven't* been able to capture the dog moving a single step with the toy in their mouth, you can skip game 12 and move straight on to game 13.

Game 12:

Follow and stop

You might think that standing still while holding the toy is easier for a dog than moving with the toy, but in most cases it isn't. Many dogs will automatically spit the toy out the moment they come to a standstill. In this game you are going to use your event marker to capture the brief moment after the dog comes to a standstill, and before they drop the toy. We'll then build on that moment to create a two-second hold.

Game goal

- The dog walks towards you as you step back, and stops when you stop, holding on to the toy for two seconds until you click.

Game overview

In the previous game, to encourage the dog to follow you with the toy, you clicked while you and the dog were still in motion. In this game you will back away from the dog, but you will stand still before you click. This is a big deal for the dog, because when *you* stand still, the dog will stop moving, and in many dogs this is the point at which they let go of the toy. Your role in this game is to get that click in *before* the dog spits out the toy. Once you have captured this moment a few times, you'll begin to build on it and increase the duration of the dog's hold in tiny increments.

As dogs become more confident, they tend to speed up, so we'll be counting seconds as we walk backwards, rather than steps from now on.

One second is the time it takes you to say 'one thousand', naturally and without rushing, in your head.

Game preparation

You'll need your treats, a clicker and plenty of space behind you, so that you are not constantly backing into walls and corners.

Game steps

To start the game, throw a treat behind you and place the toy on the floor in front of you.

Step 1

As the dog lifts the toy, take a few steps backwards so that the dog starts to follow you, then stand still. Click the instant the dog stops moving, provided the dog still has the toy in their mouth, and give the dog a treat at your side. Repeat twice more.

Click once the dog has stopped moving provided they are still holding the toy

Step 2

As the dog lifts the toy, take a few steps back then **stand still** and count one second in your head. Provided the dog still has the toy in their mouth, click. Feed the dog at your side. Repeat once more.

Step 3

As the dog lifts the toy, take a few steps back then **stand still** and count two seconds (one thousand, two thousand). Provided the dog still has the toy in their mouth, click, then feed the dog at your side.

What might happen?

At each step in the process there is the potential for the dog to spit the toy out before you have time to click. If this happens at step 3, you'll go back and play steps 1and 2 a few times before attempting step 3 again. This principle of backing up and regrouping applies at every step in the game and at every stage in learning. It enables the dog to play catch-up and is a very effective strategy.

In step 2, if you feel that the dog is holding a bit longer but not quite making it to 'one thousand', try just getting to 'one' then 'one thou'(see the six-syllable technique in the troubleshooting section on page 211). However, some dogs find it very difficult to grasp the concept of keeping hold of the toy when they stop. And there comes a point with a persistent 'spitter' when it is best to move on to a different approach.

Moving on

When you get to the point where your dog is able to stop moving, hold the toy in their mouth for two seconds, then release the toy on hearing your click, you can skip game 13 and move straight on to game 14.

If you are unable to move on past step 2 or 3 of this game and this problem persists over several sessions and several days, then you'll play the next game in this training stage: game 13. Don't worry if you need this extra step, many dogs do and it's a fun game to play!

Game 13:
Click and catch

Click and catch is a great way to get a 'hold' started in a dog that has learned to pick up a toy from the floor but is still spitting the toy out, either immediately after picking it up, or when they stop moving. I recommend playing this game if you struggled to make progress in either game 11 or 12. Click and catch is a fun game to play and is a great way for you and your dog to practise your positive reinforcement skills. It will improve your timing and will teach your dog to briefly hold on to a toy that they have picked up from the floor.

Game goal

- The dog picks a toy up from the floor and holds on to it for one second, then releases the toy into your hand on the click.

Game overview

The beginning of this game takes your dog back to the pick-up from the floor. They've done this before so it shouldn't be too difficult to get the game started. If your dog has forgotten how to play, just go back to game 8, and get the pick-up going again before you begin.

In step 1, you'll get the dog used to picking up the toy very close to you, and to having your hand in the picture. You'll get the dog lifting and dropping the toy right in front of you while your hand is close to the toy. You'll click early to avoid the dog turning away with the toy.

In step 2, you will introduce the concept that the toy can land in your hand, rather than on the floor. This is news to your dog, so you'll need to practise a bit to give them time to take this information on board. You'll be responsible for catching the toy. You'll avoid any delay and slip your hand under the dog's mouth as soon as they lift the toy up so that the toy falls into your grasp. You'll click at the same time as you reach out with your hand, so that your hand and the click are both acting together as a paired release cue.

In step 3, you'll start to delay the appearance of your hand. At first the dog will drop the toy on the floor. But without the click there is no reward. So, you'll wait for the dog to pick up the toy again and go back to step 2. They dog will probably fail at step 3 several times, but after two or three sessions of playing this game, the dog will start to wait briefly for your hand, before releasing the toy. That's when you move on to step 4, and that is the beginning of your hold.

Failure is disappointing for your dog, so it's important not to let them fail more than two or three times in a row. The win-to-lose ratio must be high enough to sustain the dog's motivation. As each dog is different, I can't tell you exactly what that ratio will be for your dog, but I suggest you start with at least three wins for every fail.

Game preparation

For this game you need to be really close to your dog so that your hand does not have to travel far, and so that you can easily grasp the toy as the dog releases it. You'll sit on a low chair or the floor if that's not too distracting for them, so that you can stretch out your hand and place it just under the dog's mouth.

Game steps

Throw a treat away from you while you place the toy on the floor right in front of you

Step 1: Close-up lifts

Position your hand low down, near the toy. As the dog lifts the toy, click and throw a treat for the dog to collect while you reposition the toy if necessary. Repeat 5–10 times

Step 2: Click and catch

As the dog lifts the toy, click as you slip your hand under their mouth. Catch the toy as they release it, throw a treat away from you, and place the toy back on the floor. Repeat ten times during the first session, then three times thereafter.

Left Have your hand low down and ready to catch to begin with
Right Reach out as the dog lifts the toy

Step 3: Let the toy fall

As the dog lifts the toy, do not put your hand under their mouth. Instead, count 'one thousand' in your head. If the dog drops the toy before you finish counting 'one thousand', go back to step 2. If the dog holds the toy for one second, slip your hand under the dog's mouth and click. Catch the toy as they release it, throw a treat away from you, and place the toy back on the floor.

Step 4

Wait for the hand

Repeat step 3 until the dog reliably holds the toy until you click. Don't worry if this feels a bit messy and awkward to begin with. You will need to practise a bit to get a smooth 'click and catch' going.

Wait until after the lift before reaching out

What might happen?

Each time you introduce a delay, there will initially be some failures whereby the dog drops the toy before you reach out for it. That's okay, just make sure your successes outnumber those failures. Some dogs are distracted by the fact that your hand has joined them for this game, so you may need to break step 1 down into several mini steps in which your hand joins in more gradually.

Moving on

When you have completed step 4 on three separate occasions over at least two days, you are ready to move on to game 14. You're making great progress – well done. Remember to give yourself some reinforcement too!

Game 14:

Hold 3, 2, 1

The purpose of this game is to increase the duration of the stationary hold. We're going to build on the brief hold you created in the last game. We'll do this because we need a little bit more duration to prepare your dog for future games where we add distractions and a cue to the release.

Today's game uses a technique I call '3, 2, 1'. It's a great way to introduce duration to any skill. The 3, 2, 1 technique simply asks for three repetitions that are very easy, then two repetitions that are a tiny bit harder, followed by a single repetition that is slightly harder again. After the hardest repetition we go back to three easy ones again. This builds your dog's confidence by setting them up to win and makes you both feel like superstars.

If you've played the click and catch game (see page 103), you might feel that letting the toy fall on the floor is a step backwards. But you don't need to worry about your dog dropping the toy, as the click means 'let go' even if your hand isn't there. We'll be building a nice delivery-to-hand at the next training stage.

Game goal

- The dog holds on to the toy for three seconds while you stand or sit in front of them.

Game overview

In this game the toy falls on the floor, not into your hand. You'll place the toy on the floor while the dog is collecting a treat. You'll then wait for the dog to lift the toy and count 'one thousand' in your head, then you'll click and throw another treat. You'll do this three times. In the second step you'll be asking for a two-second hold, so counting 'one thousand, two thousand'. And in the final step a three-second hold. You'll click when you finish counting provided the dog is still holding on to the toy. Don't worry if the dog drops the toy before you get to three seconds; this helps them learn that they need to hold on until the click or there is no reward. Just play the game again from step 1. We only ask for the three-second hold once in each game, so the dog is still winning overall.

Game preparation

You don't need to catch the toy so you can be standing up or sitting.

Game steps

Throw a treat to occupy your dog while you place the toy on the floor.

Step 1

As the dog picks up the toy, count 'one thousand' (in your head), then click. Give the dog a treat after they drop the toy and wait for them to pick up the toy again. Repeat twice more.

Jumping for joy is okay, but counting starts when all four paws hit the floor

Step 2

As the dog picks up the toy, count 'one thousand, two thousand' (in your head), then click. Repeat once more.

Step 3

As the dog picks up the toy, count 'one thousand, two thousand, three thousand' (in your head), then click. Do not repeat, instead play the game again from step 1.

One thousand, two thousand, three thousand, click!

What might happen?

This is usually a fairly trouble-free game. If your dog is finding this difficult, the most likely cause is that you've moved on to this game a bit quickly. The previous games introduce the concept of a brief hold, and without that brief hold you will find it difficult to add duration.

For some dogs, you may find it helpful to break step 1 down into three mini steps in which you count 'one', then 'one thou', then finally 'one thousand'. Turn to page 213 in the troubleshooting chapter for more information. If in doubt go back and practise the previous game for a couple of days, before coming back to this one.

Moving on

When your dog is successful at holding for three seconds and has done this on several occasions over a period of at least two days, it's time to move on to game 15.

Game 15:
Hold and tap

You now have a dog that will pick up their toy, hold the toy in their mouth for three seconds and drop the toy when you click. That is quite an achievement! In fact some of the world's most titled and successful retriever trainers are unable to do what you can do without using force or pain. Nothing you do in this course from this point on will be as challenging as your achievement so far. You should be very proud of yourself. But we want more.

You could be pretty sure that if you reached out your hand to your dog during the two-second hold you built in the last game, they would drop the toy before your hand got anywhere near it. We don't want that to happen because one of the components of our finished 'fetch' is the part where the dog holds on to the toy until you are ready to receive it. So our next task is to teach the dog that your hand is *not* a release cue. At the moment, that role belongs to your clicker. Later it will be a verbal cue, but for now, the only point at which the dog should let go of that toy is the moment they hear your click.

Game goal

- The dog holds on to the toy while you tap it, only releasing on your click.

Game overview

In this game you are going to gently tap the toy while the dog holds on to it. To begin with you just make very small movements with your hands. You then gradually increase those movements and bring them closer to the dog, while reinforcing the dog for holding on until the click.

Each repetition consists of the dog picking up the toy and holding it while you make some movements with your hands. The point at which you click varies from one step to the next. The dog must not let go until the click. After the click you'll give the dog a treat and wait for the dog to pick up the toy again.

In step 1, imagine you are brushing a crumb off your sweatshirt. If that's too much for the dog, just move one finger. We want the dog to ignore the hand movement, not react to it. In the first step, the click accompanies the hand movement for a few repetitions. This helps to avoid the dog spitting the toy when they see your hand coming, by focusing them on the click and treat. In later steps, the hand movement comes first and the click follows it provided the dog is still holding the toy.

The click must precede the drop. Apart from step 1, do not click until you have withdrawn your hand. And do not click if the dog drops the toy; wait for the dog to pick up the toy again. If the dog fails twice in a row, go back to the previous step for a few repetitions. The dog is most likely to drop the toy at steps 4 and 5. So each time you have successfully tapped the toy, go back and do some reps where you just move your hand. This helps to keep the dog's confidence and success rate high.

Game preparation

Have your treats and clicker to hand. Keep your hands close to your body unless the game instructions say otherwise.

Game steps

Throw a treat for the dog to collect while you place the toy on the floor. When you play a second time, start at step 2.

Step 1: Hand and click

As the dog picks up the toy and turns to look at you, move your non-clicker hand a very small amount at exactly the same time as you click. Give the dog a treat. Repeat several times.

Make sure the dog is focused on you with a nice secure hold before attempting to tap the toy

Step 2: Hand then click

As the dog picks up the toy and turns to look at you, briefly move your non-clicker hand a very small amount, then follow that movement with a click. Give the dog a treat. Repeat several times.

Step 3: Towards the toy

Repeat steps 1 and 2 but this time move your hand in the direction of the toy, then bring your hand back in again and click. Don't move your hand more than halfway between you and the toy. Repeat several times.

Step 4: Touch the toy

Repeat step 3 but this time touch the toy very lightly and briefly, then bring your hand back in again and click. Repeat twice.

Tap the toy very lightly to begin with

Step 5: Tap the toy

Repeat step 4 but this time tap the toy with your fingers then bring your hand back in again, then click.

What might happen?

The dog isn't paying attention

Unless the dog is looking at you, they won't see what you are doing with your hands. Usually, the previous game (14) is enough to keep your dog watching you and waiting for the cue to let go of the toy and receive their treat. But some dogs may turn away from you while they are holding the toy. If this happens, let your dog drop the toy and learn that there is no reward unless they are paying attention to you. Then play game 14 for the rest of this session and try this game again later.

The dog drops the toy when you move your hand

If the dog spits out the toy on the hand movement when you delay the click, go back and make the hand movement smaller. Find a hand movement small enough that the dog doesn't spit out the toy. It could be just moving a single finger, then build on that gradually.

The dog drops the toy after you touch it

If the dog spits out the toy after you touch or tap it in step 4 or 5 and before you click, it's tempting to rush your click in sooner. In fact, you need to slow down. Let the dog drop the toy a couple of times to learn that this doesn't work, then go back to step 3 and build a pause in between withdrawing your hand and clicking. Remember, its okay to let the dog fail, as long as you ensure that the dog experiences a good run of successes after a fail or two. If you have any problems, turn to page 216 in the troubleshooting chapter.

Moving on

Finishing this stage in training is a big achievement. In the next game we are going to start teaching your dog the cues that will enable you to work together as a team.

Stage 4:
Delivery and cues

About the cues

You now have a dog that will take pick up a toy from the floor, hold it for a few seconds, even while you reach out and touch it, then release the toy on your click. That's fantastic! Now we can start to teach the dog the all-important cues that put the fetch game in your control and allow you to remain in charge throughout. The games in this section will also prepare you for the following stage where we take our project outdoors and start playing fetch for real.

You've got several different goals to meet in this section. You need to:

Teach your dog to carry the toy towards you

Teach your dog a verbal 'let go' cue

Teach your dog a fetch cue

Teach your dog not to pick up the toy unless they hear that fetch cue

There's quite a bit to get through and it may take you a week or two to work through this section. First, let's take a closer look at those cues.

Cues as labels and triggers

In dog training a cue is a signal that is followed by an action, for example, we expect our recall whistle to be followed by the happy sight of our dog running towards us. The whistle is the cue and the recall is the required action. A reliable response to cues is what separates trained dogs from untrained dogs. In modern training, we teach the dog the cue as a label first. We do this by giving the cue when there is a very high chance that the dog is about to carry out the behaviour we want.

You will say the word 'fetch', for example, *just before* the dog is about to pick up the toy in the context of our game. We then reinforce the dog for following that cue with the action we are looking for, and, of course, we only reinforce the dog *if* they take that action. It's your job to make sure that the dog cannot engage in any other rewarding activity after ignoring a cue. This is important. It's very hard for dogs to learn the correct response if we allow them to be reinforced for doing something else after hearing or seeing our cues.

Cues remain vulnerable throughout a dog's life. If they are used when the dog is unlikely to respond in the way that we want, cues lose their meaning. At first, we use the cue repeatedly in situations where we are 99 per cent certain the dog cannot fail. And *only* in those situations. The cue then becomes strongly associated with the action we want to label, and the dog starts to understand exactly what that label means.

To get to the point where our dog will obey the cue under a wide range of normal circumstances and conditions, we need to 'put the behaviour on cue', and we need to 'proof' it. Let's take a look at each of these concepts in turn.

Putting a behaviour on cue

Giving labels to the behaviours we teach our dogs, and helping dogs to practise responding correctly to those labels, is only part of the process of teaching an effective cue. We also want the dog to be able to discriminate between our cue, and the other cues they hear from time to time. So for example, you don't want your dog to sit when you say 'fetch', or to fetch when you say 'sit'. You want them to know which behaviour to carry out when they hear each label.

In other words you want the dog: **not to fetch unless you say 'fetch', and not to to do anything other than fetch when you say 'fetch'**. This is what behaviourists mean by 'putting a behaviour on cue'.

Proofing your cues

Responding to cues is easy for the dog in certain situations. Partly because the context gives the game away. If you've just thrown a ball, you probably aren't going to tell your dog to get in their bed! And when you are playing specific games involving a toy on the floor each day, your dog will be confident that you want them to pick up the toy. When you change the context, your dog will struggle to understand what is expected of them. This is normal.

Dogs also struggle to respond correctly to cues in new situations if they are distracted. To help dogs learn easily and quickly, we design our early training set ups carefully. Real life is teeming with distractions. But in order for there to be a very high chance that the dog will take the right action after hearing the cue, in early training we are careful to keep distractions to an absolute minimum.

As training progresses, we begin to add the normal distractions of everyday life back into the equation, one at a time. And we do this for each new cue that we teach. We call this process of teaching your dog that their new cues apply in multiple locations, and in the presence of distractions, 'proofing' your cue.

A verbal fetch cue can be accompanied by a hand signal indicating the direction of the retrieve

The let go cue

Up until now, our clicker (or verbal 'yes') has functioned as the let go cue in addition to its role as a marker. We don't want to be carrying a clicker around forever, so it's time to choose a more appropriate cue to tell the dog to let go of the toy. You need to pick a cue that will work well for you, and that may depend to some extent on your interests. Certain dog sports have traditional let go cues and you might find that choosing one of these will help you feel more at home in that community. In Schutzhund and obedience competitions, the cue 'out' is common. In hunting circles the cue 'dead' is widely used. Another option is 'drop' or 'drop it' but I prefer to use that for when I want a dog to spit out something I don't want to touch.

I use the word 'dead' as a let go cue for my retrievers and spaniels. But I can see that saying 'dead' might get you a few sideways glance at your local agility club, so it's worth thinking about an appropriate cue for your situation! It's important that cues do not sound too similar to one another. The word 'out' is no good for my dogs as it is too similar to 'get out' which is the cue I use to move dogs away from me. So I chose the cue 'thank you' for Polly. You need to decide which cue you are going to use before you begin the games in this section. You can invent your own cue if you prefer, just substitute it in each of the places where I tell you to say 'thank you'.

The fetch cue

The verbal fetch cue tells your dog to go and pick up a toy. We combine this with a hand signal to show them the way to that toy, or to identify which of several toys we want them to pick up. The word 'fetch' seems to be a pretty obvious choice here, unless you have more than one dog. I often have several dogs with me, and I want them to take it in turns to retrieve. For that reason, I usually use the dog's name as a fetch cue together with a hand signal. That avoids the free for all that could follow if I were to simply to use a cue like 'fetch'. The chances are that the cue 'fetch' will work well for you; it's what I used for Polly, and is what I'll assume you'll be using.

Switching cues

Because we already have a release cue – our click – changing to our new cue 'thank you' is a straightforward matter. Dogs learn new cues with ease. All that is required is that the dog hears the new cue ('thank you') immediately before the old cue (click) a few times, and then you'll drop the old cue, and the dog will act on the new cue alone. I'll take you through this process in game 18.

Before the cues

There's a job we need to do before we add the fetch cue. It's important that we don't rehearse the wrong behaviour, so we need to make sure that we have the correct set of actions in place. We want the dog to understand that fetch means: carry out this sequence of actions in this order:

Go to the toy

Pick it up

Bring it back to me

Hold on to it until I say let go

We've mastered 1, 2 and 4 so all that remains is to get the dog returning with the toy, and then put the whole sequence together. We'll start by linking the follow and the hold. Let's get to it!

Game 16:

Follow and hold

In stage 4 we're going to be adding cues and we want to add those cues to some nice, polished behaviours. This game combines several parts of our retrieve chain: picking up a toy, following you with a toy, and holding the toy while you touch and tap it. The game strengthens your dog's hold and the association between that hold and the act of moving towards you.

Game goals

- The dog holds on to the toy and follows you with it when you back away.
- The dog brings the toy close enough for you to touch it.
- The dog continues to hold the toy, even when you touch it, until you click.

Game overview

In the first step you'll stand close to the toy and back away after the pick-up to get the dog moving towards you before you stand still again and touch and tap the toy.

In step 2 you'll add a couple of seconds to the part where your dog follows you. And a two-second wait after you touch the toy and before you take it from the dog. When they stop moving, the dog needs to be near to you. If you can't easily reach the toy, you need to back away a little more, get them moving again, then stop when they are close to you.

In step 3 we make the part where your dog follows you, and the waiting part, a bit longer. You can take it up to five seconds if you have space. Once your dog is able to follow you for three or four seconds, you may be able to turn your back on the dog as they pick up so that you don't have to walk backwards. I like to teach my puppies to follow me around the island in my kitchen carrying a toy. It's not essential, but it's good practice.

Game preparation

You'll need wear a treat bag, so you can move around freely. It's important to feed the dog right up close to you to emphasise this is the finishing position.

Game steps

Throw a treat away from you while you place the toy on the floor in front of you.

Step 1

Step back as the dog picks up the toy, stopping when the dog moves towards you. When the dog is within reach, touch the toy briefly, click and feed. Wait for the dog to pick up the toy again.

Holding while you touch the toy

Step 2

Step back as the dog picks up the toy. Keep stepping back slowly until the dog moves towards you. Get the dog following you for a couple of seconds then stop. Touch the toy briefly, **wait two seconds**, click and feed. Wait for the dog to pick up the toy again. Play at this level until the dog is succeeding repeatedly.

Step 3

Step back as the dog picks up the toy. Keep stepping back so that the dog has to **carry the toy for at least three seconds** before they reach you. Tap the toy, **wait three seconds**, click and feed. Wait for the dog to pick up the toy again.

Holding for three seconds before you take delivery

What might happen?

The dog is too far from you when they stop

It can take a little bit of practice for the dog to realise they need to catch up with you if they want to earn the click and treat. If the dog stops out of your reach, do not click. Instead, take a couple more steps back. When the dog is close enough for you to reach the toy, touch it, click and feed.

The dog drops the toy when they stop

If the dog drops the toy when they stop or before they stop, you'll need to wait for them to pick up the toy and start backing away again. If this happens more than a few times, go back and play the hold and tap game (see page 111) a few times before trying this game again. If the dog is holding briefly in step 2 but not making it to the full two seconds, make that pause a bit shorter for a few repetitions before trying again.

The dog drops the toy when you reach out

If the dog drops the toy when you reach out to touch it, wait for them to pick it up again. If this keeps happening, you need to practise the hold and tap game some more before coming back to this one. It's important at this early stage to get the dog used to holding on to that toy *right up until the click*, even when you touch or tap it, or just reach your hand in their direction.

Moving on

When your dog can comfortably carry the toy towards you for at least three seconds, hold on to it while you tap and carry on holding it while you pause for another three seconds, then release it on your click, you are ready for the next game.

Game 17:

Return and deliver

A retrieve is not complete without the safe delivery of the toy. Your dog now has a long history of dropping the toy on the floor on hearing your release cue. That's about to change. We're going to teach your dog to deliver the toy safely into your hand. We'll put this together with the understanding that bringing the toy all the way back to you is part of the deal. These two components of the delivery will complete this part of the retrieve chain and enable us to add some cues.

Game goals

- The dog holds on to the toy and returns to you with it.
- The dog releases the toy when you hold it and click.
- The dog does not release the toy when you hold it if you do not click.

Our first delivery goal is for the dog to return to you holding the toy while you stand still

Game overview

In previous games you have walked backwards to get the dog used to moving around with the fetch toy. But you don't want to be forever backing away from your dog to get them to hand over the toy, so in this game we'll introduce the concept of returning to you when you are standing still.

We begin the game by getting the dog to hold on to the toy while you grasp it. For some dogs, this is a little bit more challenging than holding the toy while you tap it. Sometimes you will take hold of the toy immediately and click so that the dog releases it into your hand. And sometimes you will grasp the toy then let go again, one or two times, before holding the toy and giving the release cue. This helps to strengthen your dog's understanding that they must not let go of the toy, even if your hand is ready to receive it, *until you give them permission* to do so.

There is no reward for the dog unless the toy ends up in your hand, so the dog needs to get close enough to you for that to happen. In step 2, you will take a few steps back from the toy while the dog is occupied collecting a treat. The idea is to put some space between you and the toy so that the dog has to carry the toy to you. This needs to happen without the visual trigger of you walking away, so you will stand still while your dog returns to you. It will take your dog a few attempts to figure out what you want them to do.

In step 3, you'll increase the distances between you and the toy, so that the dog has to travel a little further during the return.

Game preparation

You need to keep your treats on you during this game. You'll feed twice after each delivery. The first treat is delivered at your side, because that's where we want the dog to end up, and the second is thrown to occupy the dog while you put the toy on the floor.

There are quite a lot of movements to coordinate in this game, so I suggest you have a dry run or two without the dog. Just imagine the dog is in front of you and run through the actions you need to take as you move through the steps.

Game steps

Throw a treat behind you to occupy the dog while you place the toy on the floor

Step 1: Grasp and wait

Wait for the dog to pick up the toy and return with it. When the dog reaches you, grasp the end of the toy briefly and release. Wait two seconds, then grasp the toy, click and take the toy as the dog releases it. Feed one treat to the dog at your side. Throw a second treat behind you to occupy the dog while you place the toy on the floor again. Repeat twice.

Left Wait two seconds after tapping
Right Grasp the toy before you click

Step 2: Three steps

Take three steps back from the toy while the dog is collecting their treat. Take delivery of the toy as you did in step 1. Feed one treat to the dog at your side. Throw a second treat behind you while you place the toy on the floor and move away from it. Repeat once.

Step 3: Five steps

Repeat step 2 but move further back from the toy – up to five steps if space will allow. Repeat several times alternating taking the toy immediately with the 'grasp and wait' delivery on the previous page.

What might happen?

Not returning

Occasionally a dog will just stand or sit right where they picked up the toy, instead of bringing it to you. If this happens, wait ten seconds and the dog will likely start moving towards you. If they are still not close enough, back away a few steps to trigger the follow response. Again, if they drop the toy during this time, just wait for them to pick it up again.

Dropping when you take hold

It's quite likely that your dog will drop the toy the first time you take hold of one end. Even though you've been touching it and tapping it while they hold on, the dog often seems to perceive your grasp as a cue to let go. If this happens before your click, let the toy fall and wait for the dog to pick it up and try again.

Moving on

When your dog returns to you after picking up the toy, holds on to it until you click and take delivery of the toy, it's time to move on and leave the clicker behind.

Game 18:

The let go cue

Today is a big day. You are about to leave the clicker behind and move on to a proper grown-up let-go cue. Switching cues is a very straightforward process. You simply give the new cue, followed immediately by the old cue (the click), and you do this ten or twenty times, then you drop the old cue. You'll add the old cue back in a couple of times if the dog doesn't respond to the new one, but in no time at all, the dog will respond to the new cue instead and you'll be on to the next game.

Game goal

- The dog releases the toy into your hand on hearing your new let go cue.

Game overview

In step 1 you'll simply pair the two cues together. Always give the new cue first. In step 2 you'll give the dog the opportunity to let go of the toy on the new cue alone. Even if they don't do this, the gap between the two cues helps them to understand the new one.

In step 3, you'll wait for the dog to let go after the new cue only. If they don't let go, then after 30 seconds or so, you can click to get a release and go back to playing the game from step 1 again. Don't worry about putting distance between you and the toy or tapping the toy. Keep it simple, have the dog in front of you and play several times a day until the new cue is working.

Game preparation

You'll need to choose your new cue. I used the cue 'thank you' for Polly (see page 122 for more on why I chose this). Always grasp the toy *before* you give the release cue. That way the toy cannot fall on the ground. When you get to step 3 it's a good idea to put the clicker down. That way you won't click out of habit.

Game steps

Throw a treat away from you while you place the toy on the floor in front of you.

Step 1: Introduce the new cue

Wait for the dog to pick up the toy. Grasp the toy, say 'thank you' (or your chosen let go cue) followed immediately by a click. Feed the dog a treat, then throw a treat for the dog while you place the toy back on the floor. Repeat 5–10 times.

Cue 'thank you' immediately before you click

Step 2: Make a gap

Wait for the dog to pick up the toy, grasp the toy, say 'thank you', pause for 2 seconds, and if the dog has not released the toy, click. Feed the dog a treat, then throw a treat for the dog while you place the toy back on the floor. Repeat 5–10 times.

Step 3: Drop the old cue

Wait for the dog to pick up the toy, grasp the toy, say 'thank you', and wait for the dog to release the toy into your hand. Feed the dog a treat.

What might happen?

What if you drop the toy? It happens. Sometimes you give the dog the cue, you think your hand is in place, but the toy slips from your grasp. Don't pick it up! I know it was your fault, but still, the dog's job is to pick things up, you job is to receive them. Just wait for the dog to pick up the toy and take delivery of it with your new cue, 'thank you'.

Moving on

There's no need to spend long on this game. As soon as the dog has had a couple of sessions hearing the word 'thank you' (or whatever cue you have chosen for the release) and letting go of the toy afterwards, it's time to move on to the next game.

Game 19:
The long line

In the next stage of training we'll be taking our games outside. This is exciting for you, and, of course, it's exciting for your dog too, because outside is where the greatest distractions lie. It will be more important than ever that you ensure all reinforcements come from you, and that the dog is not able to help themselves to rewarding experiences, such as running around with the toy in their mouth or chasing butterflies. For this reason it makes sense with many dogs to begin outdoor training with the dog wearing a long line, sometimes referred to as a training leash. I just want to quickly explain the principles of using a training leash, talk about when and when not to use a leash, and give you a few simple guidelines to prevent potential problems. We'll be attaching the leash to your dog while they hold on to their toy. This will help to strengthen your dog's ability to hold the toy during distractions.

Using a long line/training leash

The purpose of the long line is to ensure that you can prevent the wrong behaviours being accidentally reinforced. You'll be able to pick up the end of the long line to prevent the dog leaving your 'zone of control' if they become distracted.

The long line

A long line or training leash is usually made from strong material that doesn't tangle easily. Biothane is a popular choice, and a biothane leash can be flat or cylindrical. I prefer the latter. Strong webbed fabric can work well, and if you have nothing else available, two or three rope leads tied securely together will suffice. You'll need a dog clip at one end. You won't need a very long line to begin with – three metres is fine, but it must be strong enough to keep your dog safe.

Leash safety

When you pick up a trailing line attached to a dog that is travelling at any speed, there is potential for accidental injury. It's important to make sure that the leash is attached to a collar or harness that cannot tighten around the dog's body – do not use any slip leads or running nooses of any kind. A strong buckled-up leather or webbing collar, or better still a body harness, is essential.

Leash awareness

If you use a long line like a regular leash, and keep taking hold of it, the dog will be only too aware that there is no opportunity for them to do their own thing. And they will behave differently when the leash is taken off – this is called being 'leash aware'. To avoid that happening, you'll allow the long line to trail at all times and leave it completely alone except when you need to intervene.

Game goals

- The dog holds the toy while you attach or detach a leash to their collar or harness.
- The dog releases the toy into your hand on hearing your release cue.

Game overview

Just as in the previous game, your dog must not release the toy until they hear your new release cue. You'll add some distractions into the game, but this time, instead of touching the toy, you'll be touching the dog and building up in stages to attaching a leash.

We won't ask your dog to do anything other than simple holds in this game. We want them to get used to the leash being attached and unattached, and to get used to the feel of it before we ask them to start moving around with it on.

Before we dive in and attach the leash, we'll make sure that the dog can hold on to the toy while we grasp their collar.

Game preparation

Make sure your dog is wearing a strong collar or harness and have your long line to hand. You will not need a clicker for this game, instead you'll use your new verbal 'let go' cue from now on.

Game steps

Throw a treat away from you while you place the toy on the floor in front of you.

Step 1: Pat the dog

Wait for the dog to pick up the toy, pat the dog gently and briefly on the top of their head, then grasp the toy, say 'thank you', take the toy from the dog and give the dog a treat from your hand. Now throw a second treat for the dog while you place the toy back on the floor. Repeat three times.

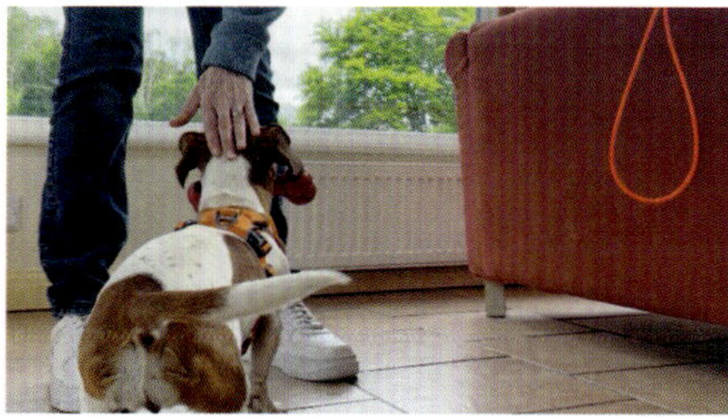

Start by patting the dog gently and briefly on the head while they are holding the toy

Step 2: Collar grab

Wait for the dog to pick up the toy, grasp the dog's collar gently and briefly. Release the collar, then grasp the toy, say 'thank you', take the toy from the dog and give the dog a treat from your hand. Now throw a second treat for your dog while you place the toy back on the floor. Repeat twice, grasping the collar more firmly.

Next practise grasping the dog's harness while they hold onto the toy

Step 3: Attach the leash

Wait for the dog to pick up the toy, attach the leash, then grasp the toy, say 'thank you', take the toy from the dog and give the dog a treat from your hand. Now throw a second treat for the dog while you place the toy back on the floor.

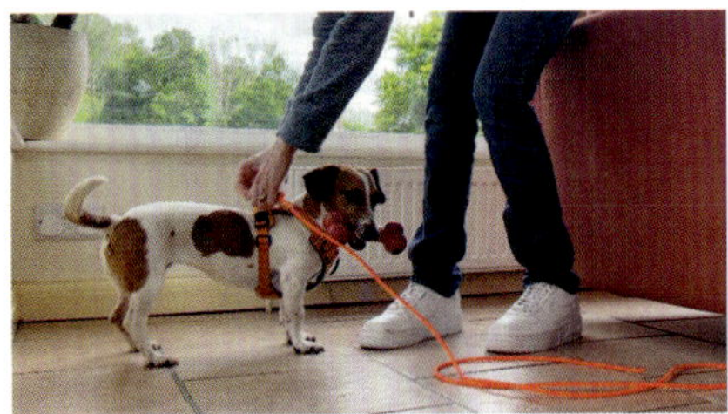

And finally attach the leash

Step 4: Remove the leash

Repeat the game from step 1, this time removing the leash in step 3.

What might happen?

Some dogs may drop the toy when you add the distractions of the pat, the collar grab or the leash. These dogs will need this game breaking down into smaller steps.

The dog drops the toy when patted

If your dog drops the toy when you touch the top of their head or their collar, wait for them to pick up the toy, then make smaller hand movements to begin with just as you did in the hold and tap game (see page 111).

The dog drops the toy while you are attaching the leash

You may need to put an extra step in between steps 2 and 3. For example, you may need a step where you simply dangle the leash next to the dog and remove it again.

The dog doesn't like the line

Signs that the dog doesn't like wearing the line include a reluctance to pick up the toy while the line is attached. These games should always be fun for your dog. If the fun stops when the dog is wearing the long line, you need to consider whether or not to continue with it. For most dogs, the long line is an optional extra. It's a useful tool to prevent dogs self-reinforcing in distracting environments. Some dogs find a long line rather inhibiting. Polly is one of these dogs, and as we were only playing these games at home, in our fenced garden, she is not usually wearing one. If the long line is essential because you don't have a safe outdoor space to play with your dog, or because your dog is very distractible, then you may need to spend some time getting your dog used to theirs. They may need some extra practice wearing the line outside the context of the games. For example, you can attach the line before each meal and remove it afterwards. Or they can wear the line around the house while you are there. You can also have them wear a shorter or lighter line to begin with, until they grow accustomed to the extra weight of it.

Moving on

Your dog needs to be comfortable holding the toy while you attach or remove their leash, before you move on to the next game. And if you are intending to continue to use a long line going forwards, your dog also needs to be comfortable with it and happy to pick up the toy while they are wearing it. In the next game we are going to teach your dog the fetch cue.

Game 20:

The fetch cue

We've talked about what it means to put a behaviour on cue. Part of that process involves teaching your dog not to fetch without that all-important cue. So what we want to achieve next is for you to be able to place a toy on the floor and have the dog wait for your permission to pick it up, rather than doing so automatically. We'll be introducing the cue 'fetch' and using it in a simple game that combines and develops the skills your dog has learned so far. And if you've decided to use a long line in your outdoor training sessions you will be attaching it before each session from now on. This helps prevent your dog becoming 'leash aware' outdoors.

Game goals

- The dog hears the word 'fetch' before each pick-up.
- The dog holds the toy even when you grasp it.
- The dog releases the toy when you say 'thank you'.

Game overview

In today's game we'll practise some simple retrieves as we introduce the new fetch cue. We introduce our new cue by giving the cue immediately before the dog picks up the toy. At first this new cue is just noise. It doesn't have any meaning for the dog and may even distract them from making the pick-up. So don't worry if the dog turns back to you when they hear your cue. Just keep still and wait for them to return to the toy.

You'll be throwing a treat behind you as you place the toy in front of you, so that the dog is running past you and away from you when they pick up the toy. In step 1 you'll keep the distances short. In step 2 you'll put more space between you and the toy by walking backwards after dropping the toy in front of you. You'll say 'fetch' after the dog has collected their treat and, ideally, just as the dog makes visual contact with the toy.

Game preparation

You'll need to wear a treat bag and have as much space behind and in front of you as possible. Remember to attach your long line (unless you have decided not to use one) before this and all future games even the indoor ones.

When you use a verbal cue it's important to try to make the cue as clear and consistent as possible. You can practise the way you want your fetch cue to sound without your dog first.

Game steps

Step 1: Short fetch

Throw a treat behind you while you place the toy on the floor in front of you and take a step back.

Just before the dog reaches the toy, say 'fetch'. Wait for the dog to return with the toy, then grasp the toy, say 'thank you' and give the dog a treat. Repeat up to ten times.

Your arm points the way to the toy

Step 2: Longer fetch

Throw a treat behind you while you throw the toy in front of you and take several steps back

As the dog passes you, say 'fetch' and keep stepping back until the dog reaches the toy. Wait for the dog to return with the toy, then grasp the toy, say 'thank you' and give the dog a treat. Repeat up to ten times.

What might happen?

There's not much can go wrong with this game. Remember to let the dog pick up the toy if you drop it. You can increase the distance in step 2 as your space allows – a hall or corridor can help here. And you can build your dog's confidence and understanding of the word 'fetch' by playing in different parts of your training area and in different parts of your home. Make retrieves very short and simple when you change your location and avoid all distractions.

Moving on

You don't need to spend hours on this game. It's just about your dog hearing the cue, so that the cue becomes familiar, and understanding that the cue means pick up the toy, bring it to me, hold it until I say 'thank you', and let go immediately on my cue. In the games to come, your dog will learn *not* to fetch *unless* they hear the cue. Play this game a few times over a couple of days, then move on straight on to training stage 5.

Stage 5: **The wait**

Fetching on cue

Your dog has now begun to associate the word 'fetch' with collecting a toy and delivering it safely into your hand. You are making great progress! In this section we are going to deepen your dog's understanding of what the fetch cue means. We are pursuing the aim of putting the fetch behaviour 'on cue', so we need your dog to:

Fetch when they hear the fetch cue

Not fetch when they don't hear the fetch cue

Not fetch when they hear a different cue

We'll be playing games that support those aims. Perhaps the biggest and most exciting goal for this stage in training is to start making the transition to playing fetch outdoors in the real world. We'll also be working on your dog's sit-stay and using some other cues to help keep your dog engaged, as well as some techniques to enable you to remain in control in this new environment. There are some challenges ahead, but you are well prepared to meet them.

Generalising cues

Indoors, in your usual training area, if you say 'fetch' and there's a toy nearby, your dog will likely pick it up. But dogs are very poor at generalising cues. So when we go outside, we may need to repeat some of our training in this new environment. We don't usually have to go right back to the beginning, but we do need to simplify things until the dog has learned to focus on the games in this new and more distracting training area. Young dogs are particularly poor at paying attention when there are exciting things to watch and see, but their ability to pay attention around distractions is a bit like a muscle; it gets stronger with use. We can build this muscle by asking the dog to carry out simple tasks (such as giving eye contact or touching your hand) in the garden before trying to recreate our new and more complex 'fetching' behaviour in a public place such as a park.

Waiting for permission

Perhaps the hardest part of retrieve training is teaching dogs *not* to fetch until they hear your cue. As retrieves get further away and the dog has a chance to build up speed, excitement levels grow so it is important that you establish its ability to 'wait' for our cues at this early stage when your dog is relatively calm. Most of the games in this section are focused on building your dog's ability to wait for that all-important fetch cue. And that's where 'sit' comes in.

The role of 'sit' in retrieving

I like to keep the prerequisites for playing fetch to a minimum. Advanced retrieving dogs need some important obedience skills in order to be able to work as a team with a human handler, but we are not entering a competition here, we are just teaching your dog to fetch a toy and give it back so that it can be thrown again. Having said that, it is desirable that your dog doesn't fetch the toy unless you've given it the fetch cue, especially if you are going to move on to more advanced retrieving when you finish this course, and I hope you do because it's so much fun!

When you don't want your dog to fetch until you say so, it is important that the dog knows what you want them to do instead. The simplest option is usually to ask the dog to sit. This will also help us when we are positioning the toy. Up until now we've been throwing a treat to occupy the dog while the toy is placed on the floor. But as we progress, we want to be able to have the dog sit and watch as we place or even throw the toy into position.

Getting a reliable sit

Even if your dog has a basic understanding of the command 'sit', remaining seated while a toy is sailing through the air with the prospect of a chase is really hard for many dogs, so it's important not to throw the dog in at the deep end. Instead, you'll build up gradually and work on your dog's understanding of what 'sit' really means. And if you are going to use 'sit' as a means of controlling your dog during the fetch game, or in any other training context, 'sit' really does need to mean '*sit until I say you can move*'.

In many homes and families up and down the land, that is not what 'sit' means at all. It often means 'sit until you get bored' or 'sit while I give you a treat'. Even if one member of the family attempts to train a reliable sit-stay, it is common for other family members to sabotage their efforts. If sit means one thing when you say it and another when your partner or kids say it, the dog will usually give up paying attention to anyone's cue. Sometimes you can solve this by teaching your dog a special, secret sit cue, that only you use. I do something similar in that I teach my dogs to sit on the cue 'hup'. So that when well-meaning visitors say 'sit' to my dogs and then fail to follow that up with a release cue or a reward, it doesn't do my own sit cue any harm. If you don't want to do this, it's important to get other family members on board with only telling the dog to sit when they are likely to be successful, always rewarding the dog when they succeed, and always remembering to release the dog. If the dog gets up without hearing a release cue, then they don't understand what 'sit' means, and they won't be able to sit for very long in a distracting situation.

Leash and long line

All of the games in this section will be played outdoors and some of them will be played indoors first. Unless you have decided to dispense with the long line for now, you'll need to attach a long line to your dog's harness or collar before each training session. It's important that you do this for the indoor sessions too. Not because they need the long line indoors, but because you don't want the dog to perceive the lack of a long line as an opportunity for them to do their own thing.

At times, you'll also have your dog on a leash. This is useful in some of our fetch games to lead the dog away from a toy that has been placed, and to restrain the dog during some exercises that require a more advanced sit-stay than your dog might have achieved so far. We don't use the long line to walk the dog around, because we don't want the dog to be aware of it, or to think about it.

This means that sometimes, the dog will have both a leash and a long line fastened to their collar or harness at the same time. If the rings or attachment points on your harness or collar are not big enough for this purpose, you can attach a loop of string or thin rope to the dog's collar and clip the leash and the long line to that.

Chasing a toy without permission is known as running in, and there are disadvantages to letting your dog do this

Game 21:

The hand touch

The hand touch game will help get your dog focused on you outdoors. It will also help your dog discriminate between different cues. Dogs really enjoy this game and pick it up very quickly. It's a great way to get your dog to focus on you when you begin training in new locations, and test whether your dog is calm enough to train in that situation. You'll start the game off indoors, and once you've added the cue, you'll take the game outside.

Your outdoor training space

You need to pick your outdoor training location carefully to minimise distractions and interruptions – your own back garden is usually the best place to start because you can control those two factors. If you don't have a garden, then a safe recreation area visited at unsociable hours will often enable you to train in peace. If you are going into a public area or an area that isn't secure, you'll need to have the dog wear a long line. If you are going to use a long line, remember to attach the line for the indoor games too.

Game overview

You will start by holding the palm of your hand facing towards the dog, about 5–10cm from the dog's nose so they can easily reach forwards and touch it. You'll keep your hand in that position for a few seconds, then remove it for a few seconds, then present it again. If the dog sniffs or touches the palm of your hand, you will say 'yes', remove the target hand and feed the dog.

To progress the game you'll present your hand slightly further from the dog, and in different positions so that the dog has to reach a little further and to move their body in different directions. You'll keep marking and treating the dog while requiring slightly more movement from them. After two or three sessions you'll start to include repetitions where your hand is higher, so the dog has to reach or even jump up, and others where your hand is low down near the floor. You'll also present your hand out to either side, so that the dog is having to move from side to side in front of you to keep earning treats. Once you can move your dog around by presenting your hand in different positions, you'll add the cue 'touch'.

Do not push your hand against the dog's nose or help the dog to make contact with your hand. It's the dog's choice whether or not to touch it, and as always, the right choice is reinforced, the wrong choice gets nothing.

Don't try to get through all the steps in your first session. Each time you play, start at the step before the one you finished with last time. You'll play this game indoors to begin with and once your dog is fluent at responding to the hand touch cue, you'll start to play the game outdoors.

Game preparation

You'll need a well-stocked treat bag plus a long line if you are using one. I suggest you use the verbal marker 'yes' but if your dog is struggling to get going with this, you might find the clicker helpful. You can switch the click for 'yes' once your dog gets the idea.

Game steps

Step 1: Easy touch

Present your hand about 5cm from the dog's nose. Click and give them a treat as soon as the dog touches your hand with their nose. Once the dog is repeatedly bumping your hand, increase the distance between your dog's nose and your hand up to 30cm.

Make hand touches easy to begin with

Step 2: Moving touch

Present your hand slightly to the left of the dog. Click and and give them a treat as soon as they touch your hand with their nose, then present your hand slightly to the right of the dog. Repeat alternating sides, gradually making the dog move further to each side. You can also present your hand at different heights, some low, some higher.

Ask for a little more effort as your dog gains confidence

Step 3: Add the cue

Repeat step 2 using the cue 'touch' each time you present your hand. Once you have introduced the cue, don't play again without it.

Step 4: Outdoors

Repeat step 3 in your outdoor training space.

Playing outdoors

Once your dog is fluent at the hand touch game, you can start to play the game outdoors. Use the cue 'touch' every time you present your hand. Once your dog is comfortably responding to every touch cue, start to move around and play in different parts of your garden.

What might happen?

Sometimes it can be difficult to get the dog to make the first touch. If this happens you can rub the palm of your hand with a little bit of cheese. Say 'yes' or click when the dog touches your hand to sniff it.

Some dogs will bump your hand several times in a row, and you think you've cracked it, and then they stop bumping your hand and seem confused. Don't worry, sometimes the dog needs a bit of time to think. Just rub another bit of cheese on your hand and try again. It may take two or three sessions to get past step 1 and that's fine

Occasionally a dog will lick rather than bump your hand with their nose. This is usually solved by clicking early, just before the dog actually touches you.

Moving on

When you take your dog out in public, you can play this game on a leash. Try it out in as many different locations as you can. Start with the least distracting places, and build up to environments where you know your dog finds it harder to focus. Your dog will soon be a pro. When you have played this game several times outdoors and your dog is eagerly and purposefully moving to touch your hand as soon as you present it, it's time to move on to the next game

Game 22:

Outdoor fetch

This is the moment we've been waiting for! We're going to take the fetch game outdoors now and for some dogs this is a very big deal. We'll try to make the transition as smooth as possible, and I'll explain what to do depending on your dog's reaction to this new environment. For most dogs we won't be throwing the toy yet. A moving toy is much more exciting, but our aim is to get the dog to pick up a toy that has been placed on the ground rather than thrown. This will help us build steadiness – the ability to wait for a retrieve cue, and prepare the dog for a lot of fun games that don't involve a moving toy.

Game goal

- The dog picks up a toy placed on the ground outdoors on hearing your cue 'fetch'.

Game overview

How this game goes will depend on your dog. You'll start in step 1 with a few simple pick-ups and deliveries indoors. You'll drop a treat behind you and place the toy on the floor in front of you, cue 'fetch' as the dog returns from collecting their treat, and take delivery of the toy. You'll repeat this a couple of times and then without a break, you'll go straight on to step 2 which is when you take the dog outside. If you have different surfaces in your outdoor space (paving, gravel, grass) then you'll need to practise on each different surface.

Many dogs will behave exactly the same outside as they did inside but some may be reluctant to pick up the toy on one or more of the outdoor surfaces. If this happens, you will tease the dog with the toy and throw it, allowing the dog to chase it and bring it back. Once they have retrieved the toy a few times, you can make the throws shorter and shorter until the dog will pick up the toy from your feet.

Each time the dog returns with the toy, wait briefly before you take delivery of the toy. You don't need to worry about tapping and touching the toy provided the dog is reliably holding the toy until you take it. But the dog must present the toy to you and not drop it before the release cue. If either of you drops the toy, wait for the dog to pick it up again. Getting the toy into your hand is their job now.

Game preparation

Remember to attach the long line before the indoor game if you are using one. And make sure your dog has had a chance to pee before you play the indoor game so that you won't be interrupted by the call of nature when you head outside. Prepare plenty of your dog's favourite treats. High-value treats are especially important when moving into a new environment.

Game steps

Step 1: Indoors

Throw a treat behind you while you place the toy on the floor in front of you.

Before the dog reaches the toy, give your cue 'fetch'. Wait for the dog to return with the toy, then take delivery of the toy and give the dog a treat. Repeat a couple of times then take the dog outdoors

Play a few times indoors just before you go outside

Step 2: Hard surface outdoors

Throw a treat behind you while you place the toy on a paved area in front of you.

Before the dog reaches the toy, give your cue 'fetch'. Wait for the dog to return with the toy, then take delivery of the toy and give the dog a treat. Repeat several times, until the dog is responding quickly each time.

Play on a hard surface first if you have one

Step 3: Outdoor grass

Repeat step 2 on grass several times and until the dog is responding quickly each time.

Practise this game two or three times a day, for at least two days, moving from indoors to out, until your dog is confidently picking up the toy each time no matter where they are.

What might happen?

Some dogs can be a little confused by being asked to fetch outside. I mentioned 'teasing' the dog in the game overview; this means wiggling the toy along the ground in front of the dog, or gently pushing it against them and snatching it away, whichever they find the most exciting. Tease a little bit then move the toy quickly from side to side, and as soon as the dog starts to focus on the toy, throw it.

Take delivery of the toy just as you normally would then tease and throw again. Repeat two or three times then go straight into step 2, with a treat behind and the toy on the ground. You may have to tease and throw a few more times – make these throws shorter and shorter until the dog is picking up in front of you.

Occasionally a dog will be unimpressed with 'tease and throw'. In which case you can start off by verbally marking the dog ('yes') for any kind of interaction with the toy, such as a glance. Then build up to a touch and a pick-up with delivery. It doesn't take long to catch up to where you were indoors with a dog that's successfully learned to pick up indoors.

Moving on

Play this game until your dog fetches the toy you place on the ground on any kind of surface. This achievement is a major milestone, you are now almost ready for the five great fetch games in the final stage of training. All that remains is a little work on that nice steady sit-stay. So let's get to it!

Game 23:

The sit

For most dogs, their instinct when you throw a toy, is to chase after it. In order to teach your dog only to retrieve when they hear your fetch cue, we need to give the dog an alternative to chasing. And that alternative is the sit. Most people with a dog over six months old have already taught their dog to sit. Not many have taught the dog not to get up again without permission.

This game helps your dog to understand that every sit has duration, that *you* get to decide how long that duration is and that their job is to listen up for your instructions. For some dogs, this game may take a few days to master. There's no retrieving involved in this game. So, set aside an extra few minutes each day to practise outdoor fetch, in addition to your 'sit' session.

How to end the sit

From now on, you'll always end the sit with a cue, rather than just leaving the dog to drift away on their own initiative. It's also important that you end the sit after an appropriate length of time, one where your dog has a good chance of succeeding. And you need to build duration up gradually, starting with just a second or two. The 3,2,1 principle (see page 107) works well here: three repetitions of an easy sit, a couple that are slightly harder, then just one repetition of a slightly longer sit before returning to easy ones again.

We can end the sit in one of two ways: a dog can be released with a release cue, such as a click or word, which ends the behaviour; or we can give the dog another job to do, such as a hand touch or a retrieve. If you don't already have a verbal release cue for your sit, now is the time to introduce one. I use 'okay', but words like 'free', and 'break' are also popular.

Feeding during the sit

When we add duration, we can do so in two ways. We can increase duration very gradually, like you did with the hold, or we can feed during the duration. Obviously, that wouldn't work with hold, but it works well with the sit. In step 1 of this game we feed the dog just after the sit cue, and again just before the release.

Game goal

- The dog sits on cue outdoors and remains seated while you leave the dog and return.

Game overview

This game is about establishing that your dog can sit still for a few seconds and during a few simple distractions. And that they can do this in your outdoor training area. You'll introduce duration first because all distractions involve duration. And if your dog cannot sit still for five seconds, with you close at hand, they certainly won't be able to sit still while you leave them.

Each step is one we would normally cover in several different games with a puppy or very young dog. Depending on how far you have got with training your dog you may need to break down these steps further. I'll give you an example of how to do this after the game steps. You'll work through all the steps indoors before taking the game outside.

Game preparation

If your dog needs a long line outdoors, make sure they wear the long line on the indoor sessions too. To practise your dog's hold, just before you start the game, you can get the dog to hold the toy while you attach the line.

Game steps

Throw a treat away from you to start the game.

Step 1: Five-second sit

When the dog returns, cue 'sit' and feed the dog. Count five seconds in your head. Feed the dog again. Cue 'okay' to release the dog and throw a treat.

Step 2: Marching sit

When the dog returns cue 'sit'. Feed the dog, then march on the spot five times. Feed the dog again. Cue 'okay' to release the dog and throw a treat.

Step 3: Turnaround sit

When the dog returns, cue 'sit'. Feed the dog, then turn in a full circle without leaving your position. Feed the dog again. Cue 'okay' to release the dog and throw a treat.

Feed in position at the beginning and end of each sit, starting indoors

Step 4: Step away sit

When the dog returns, cue 'sit'. Feed the dog and take two steps back, then two steps forwards. Feed the dog again. Cue 'okay' to release the dog and throw a treat.

Step away and return slowly, break it down into smaller steps if necessary

Step 5: Hand touch release

When the dog returns, cue 'sit'. Feed the dog, then cue 'touch' to end the sit. Give a verbal marker 'yes' as soon as the dog bumps your hand and throw a treat.

Once the dog is successful at sitting throughout all the steps, take the game outdoors.

Left Repeat each of the distractions outdoors
Right Give the dog a chance to look up at your face before returning to them

What might happen?

At any point in these steps the dog could get up before you cue the end of the sit. If that happens, wait for the dog to sit again and continue. If it happens more than twice in a row, you need to make the sit easier. In step 1 you could feed the dog at one-second intervals, then at two-second intervals and so on. In step 2 you could start just by lifting one leg and putting it down again. In step 3 you could start by turning a quarter circle then turning back to face the dog. And in step 4 you could start by just placing one foot behind you.

Playing outdoors

You need to work through each of these steps again when you take the game outdoors. Once you get to step 4, you can increase your step-away distance to four or five steps. You can also create your own variations, such as turning your back on the dog and walking away instead of backing away. Start with one step and build your walk away up gradually, step by step, and return to the dog each time to treat and release them.

Moving on

True steadiness, or the ability to wait patiently while toys are flying about, takes time to establish. In the meantime, you need another way to prevent your dog from chasing while we play a variety of fetch games. So, when your dog can sit still outdoors, and watch you march, turn, move away and return without breaking the sit, it's time for the next game: the restrained fetch.

Game 24:
Restrained fetch

Now you have the basic sit-stay in place, you'll be able to start building your dog's steadiness. But first we are going to learn how to restrain a dog before they fetch a toy. We're also going to have some fun throwing toys around!

We need to be careful to maintain a balance between exciting retrieves and steadiness work. We want our dogs to be excited about playing fetch, but not so excited that they are incapable of listening to our cues. Too *much* control can put a damper on things and turn the joy into a big old chore. So your dog needs to keep experiencing the more exciting side of fetch while learning the more controlled games. And that's where restraint can help us.

Restraint (holding the dog's collar or harness) can *build* excitement as the dog tries to pull away and get to the toy. But it can also have the opposite effect. Grabbing the collar of a dog very new to retrieving outside can have the effect of shutting the dog down, so that they don't want to pick anything up. So we need to introduce restraint with care.

Game goal

- Your dog runs out to fetch a marked retrieve (a toy the dog watched you throw) on your cue when you let go of their collar.

Game overview

There are two steps to this game. You'll play the first step until the dog is chasing the toy enthusiastically then switch to the second step. If and when your dog loses their enthusiasm for running out for the toy, you'll switch back to the first step again. You'll play the whole game outdoors.

For some dogs, you'll only ever have to play the first step once; with other dogs you may need to switch back and forth quite a bit.

Game preparation

You'll need your toy, a pocket or bag to put it in, and your treats. Your dog will need to be wearing a strong buckle collar or body harness. Make sure its loose enough for you to slip your fingers underneath. You need an area of paving or short grass where the dog can clearly see the toy.

Game steps

Step 1: No restraint

Give your dog a treat, then produce the toy. Make sure you have their interest – tease or wiggle their toy about, if necessary, then cue 'fetch' and throw the toy 1.5–3m away. It needs to land in clear view.

Take delivery of the toy, put it out of sight and give the dog a treat. Repeat until the dog is running after the toy with enthusiasm.

Tease with the toy and throw a few times before attempting to restrain your dog

Step 2: Restraint

Give your dog a treat, then produce the toy. Make sure you have their interest, tease or wiggle the toy about if needs be. Grasp the dog's collar, then in quick succession, cue 'fetch', throw the toy 1.5–3m away and let go of the dog. Take delivery of the toy and give the dog a treat.

Repeat up to five times. Stop sooner if the dog shows any sign of losing enthusiasm. If the dog loses enthusiasm, go back to step 1 and next time you play, alternate restrained and unrestrained retrieves.

Top Restrain the dog by holding their collar or harness
Above Pause briefly then take delivery of the toy

What might happen?

If the dog stops short of the retrieve and comes back, they can't see it clearly enough and have lost confidence. Make the retrieves shorter next time and think about playing on a surface where the dog can see the toy more easily. If your dog finds the game easy, then you can increase the distances a little bit.

Moving on

When your dog is happily running out to the toy you just threw in clear view, even after being restrained, you are ready for the next lesson. We are going to finish off the preparations for the final stage in training with a steadiness game.

Game 25:

Steady

Now that we've established a sit response that is resistant to a little bit of distraction, we're going to teach your dog that not every toy on the floor is theirs to grab. We'll start this game off indoors, then take it outside.

Game goal

- Your dog is able to sit still while you place a toy on the ground outdoors.

Game overview

In this game your dog is going to watch what you do with the toy. All they have to do is remain sitting still. We want to make the dog aware that sitting still is a very rewarding thing to do in its own right and that fetching is only something they do when they hear that all-important fetch cue. We will make the sit as rewarding as we can by giving treats *during* the sit-stay and not just after the release.

Practise step 1 until the dog is able to sit still throughout, then the next time you play, include step 2. Don't include the next step until the dog can play reliably at the previous one. Once your dog is fluent at this game right through to step 4 indoors, you will take it outside. Stick to your usual training zone and play the game from the very beginning again.

Game preparation

You'll need a way of carrying the toy. A pocket can work, or you can tuck it under your arm. But you need to be able to present it, then remove it again. If your dog is reluctant to move from the sit after your release cue, you can feed after the release as well as during the sit.

Game steps

Step 1: Presenting the toy

Cue 'sit' and give the dog a treat. Take three steps back. Now hold the toy out to one side where the dog can see it, count two seconds, then remove it from view. Step forward and treat the dog again. Cue 'okay' to release the dog. Repeat several times

Presenting the toy

Step 2: Lowering the toy

Cue 'sit' and give the dog a treat. Take three steps back. Now hold the toy out to one side where the dog can see it. Lower the toy part-way to the ground, then lift it back up and remove it from

view. Step forwards and treat the dog again. Cue 'okay' to release the dog. Repeat three times.

Lowering the toy

Step 3: Placing the toy

Cue 'sit' and give the dog a treat. Take three steps back. Place the toy on the ground. Wait two seconds then lift it back up and remove it from view. Step forwards and treat the dog again. Cue 'okay' to release the dog. Repeat twice.

Placing the toy on the floor

Step 4: Leaving the toy

Cue 'sit' and give the dog a treat. Take three steps back. Place the toy on the ground. Leaving the toy behind, step forwards and treat the dog again. Step back and collect the toy. Return to the dog and treat them again. Now cue 'okay' to release the dog. Repeat the game from the beginning, until the dog can complete each step without breaking a sit (getting up), then take the game outside.

Leaving the toy behind

What might happen?

If the dog breaks the sit your priority is to step on the toy so that they cannot pick it up, then wait for them to sit again. If you have more than two failures in a row, always go back to a point at which the dog can succeed.

Moving on

Once your dog can reliably sit while you step back and leave a toy on the ground in your outdoor training area, it's time to move on to the final stage of our training.

Stage 6:
The retrieve

Making fetch work for you

Congratulations on making it to stage 6. What an achievement! Everything you have done in the previous training stages has been about getting you to this point. And now it's time to learn five different ways to play fetch. These are not just training games, they are also games for life. You will be able to build on them and teach your dog to play them in all kinds of different locations, and I'll give you tips for doing that in each game. The right mix of games for you and your dog will depend on what you want to get out of playing fetch, and to some extent on your dog's temperament.

Fetch can be as simple as wanting a bit of fun with your dog in the garden, a way to keep your dog fit, or it can be part of a sport or activity that you aim to participate in with your dog. Some of these sports demand higher standards of behaviour than others, particularly in terms of steadiness, so I think we should probably talk a bit more about chasing before we go any further, because it will help you decide how far you want to take the game of fetch. And whether or not you want to expend the effort that achieving and maintaining steadiness requires.

The chasing instinct

For many dogs, chasing a moving object is about as good as it gets. Some breeds, such as whippets and other sight hounds, have a passion for chasing hard-wired into their personality. Chasing is common in some other breeds too, border collies for example. Teaching these dogs NOT to chase can be

Which games you play will depend partly on how your dog feels about fetch

challenging, especially if they have a long history of chasing behind them. One of the problems is that chasing is self-reinforcing, the *act* of chasing is, in itself, rewarding.

Does it matter?

Retriever trainers have a name for chasing after a retrieve without permission. They call it 'running in'. In the UK's gundog circles, running in is considered at best a nuisance and at worst, a heinous crime. It will also put you out of any competition you enter.

But if you are not training a retriever as a hunting companion, does it really matter if your dog takes off and chases after the ball or toy as soon as you have launched it? There are some pros and cons of allowing a dog to run in on every retrieve.

Pros

Less time and effort on your part

Cons

Dog can't take turns

Risk of injury

Dog may be ineligible for some sporting activities

Loss of control

May start or worsen a chasing habit

Restricts the games you can play

Let's look at those cons in a bit more detail. Turning at speed places a lot of stress on a dog's joints. And chasing a rapidly decelerating object often involves turning at speed. In addition, two or more dogs racing and jostling for the same prize may result in collisions and even fights. Taking turns allows friends to play fetch with multiple dogs. This can be a lot of fun and a dog that won't take turns spoils that fun for the other dogs.

Consider also, that once a dog has taken off without permission they are essentially out of control until they choose to return, which may put them at further risk of accident or injury. On top of all that, the self-reinforcing nature of chasing means that it can be extremely habit-forming.

As you can see, I am in favour of teaching most dogs to wait for permission to retrieve. But it would be misleading of me if I glossed over how challenging it can be to maintain steadiness in a dog that is really wound up about retrieving, or that has been allowed to chase in the past. And more than anything, I want you to have fun with your dog.

If you have a small, compact dog, like Polly, who is less prone to joint injury, with no history of chasing problems and you have no ambitions to train your dog as a hunting companion or to compete in any kind of dog sport that involves retrieving, then it probably isn't the end of the world if your dog chases after the balls you throw. Just know that this is an easier thing to prevent than to cure.

Different ways to retrieve

There are three different types of retrieve in this final section:

Marked retrieves

Memory retrieves

Blind retrieves

Marked retrieves, where the dog sees a toy thrown and fall, are the kind of retrieve people generally think about when they talk about playing fetch. These are the games that dogs find the most exciting and that challenge steadiness. To instil and maintain steadiness in our dogs we teach them to take turns with these kinds of retrieve. You'll find them in games 26 and 29 (see page 185 and 199).

Blind and memory retrieves, where there is no visual trigger of a falling object, don't challenge steadiness in the way. They are simply not as exciting to your dog. But they are still hugely enjoyable and are great ways to develop your dog's hunting and tracking abilities and keep them fit. If you want a steady dog, then you'll need to balance the amount of time you spend on these different activities with your dog's temperament and enthusiasm for playing fetch.

Your goals

As you embark on this final stage in training your dog to play fetch, it's worth thinking about what you want to get out of retrieving. About what it means for you. Is it just a bit of fun? A way to spend time with your dog? Or do you think you might want to take fetch further?

You'll also need to consider how your dog feels about fetch and how much drive and passion they have for the various games. I'll talk some more about that in the final chapter, but essentially, the more excitable your dog is, and the harder they find sitting still, the longer you should spend on the calmer games. Let's start with one of those: game 26.

Game 26:

One for you, two for me

The retrieves in this game are all marked retrieves, so you'll make sure your dog is watching you while you put the toy out. These retrieves will be a bit more exciting than the ones in the previous 'steady' game and you'll be taking it in turns with your dog to collect the toy. This helps the dog learn to wait patiently as they start to understand that not every toy is theirs to fetch. Sometimes a person (and ultimately another dog) gets a turn. Like all the games in this section, you can carry on playing this game after you have started to play the next one.

Avoiding accidental reinforcement

It's inevitable, as training progresses, that your dog will sometimes make mistakes. It's your job to make sure the dog will not be reinforced for those mistakes. If your dog attempts to fetch without permission, you must get to the toy before it does. The simplest option is to step on the toy. Don't bend over and try to pick it up with your hands. You and the dog will end up colliding and they'll grab the toy while you are busy collecting your dignity.

Game goals

- The dog sits and waits calmly while you drop toys on to the ground and while you walk around and collect those toys.
- The dog sits and waits calmly while you drop toys on to the ground and fetches them when you give the fetch cue.

Game overview

For every marked retrieve you allow your dog to fetch, you'll create at least two other marked retrieves that your dog has to watch *you* collect. You'll start by gently placing the toy, progress to dropping the toy from shoulder height and move on to throwing the toy a short distance. The more exciting we make the toy, by throwing it faster, higher or further, the further from the dog we move. So you'll also be building your dog's ability to sit and stay at a distance.

Each time you place a toy, you'll return to the dog and grasp their collar, then give them a treat before either collecting the toy yourself or sending your dog to fetch it. The reason for the collar grab on every repetition is because we don't want the collar grab to become another cue for fetch.

Game preparation

You'll need your treat bag, the toy and your long line, if you are using one. Make sure you have somewhere safe to keep the toy out of the dog's reach when it is not placed on the ground.

Game steps

Step 1: Place the toy at three paces

TWO REPETITIONS: YOU COLLECT THE TOY.

Cue 'sit'. Feed the dog. Take three paces back and place the toy on the ground. Return to the dog, grasp the dog's collar and feed them again. Step back to collect the toy, return to the dog and feed. Cue 'okay' to release the dog. Repeat.

ONE REPETITION: THE DOG COLLECTS THE TOY.

Cue 'sit'. Feed the dog. Take three paces back and place the toy on the ground. Return to the dog and grasp the dog's collar. Point at the toy, cue 'fetch' and release the collar.

Top At three paces place the toy carefully on the ground
Middle Feed in position at the beginning of each sit
Above Polly's turn

Step 2: Drop the toy at four paces

TWO REPETITIONS: YOU COLLECT THE TOY.

Cue 'sit'. Feed the dog. Take four paces back, hold the toy out to one side at waist height, and drop it on the ground. Return to the dog and feed the dog. Collect the toy, return to the dog and feed. Cue 'okay' to release the dog. Repeat.

ONE REPETITION: THE DOG COLLECTS THE TOY.

Cue 'sit'. Feed the dog. Take four paces back, hold the toy out to one side at waist height, and drop it on to the ground. Return to the dog, grasp the dog's collar and feed them again. Point at the toy, cue 'fetch' and release the collar.

Step 3: Throw the toy at six paces

TWO REPETITIONS: YOU COLLECT THE TOY.

Cue 'sit'. Feed the dog. Take six paces back, and hold the toy out to one side while facing the dog. Gently throw it a short distance. Return to the dog, grasp the dog's collar and feed them again. Collect the toy, return to the dog and feed. Cue 'okay' to release the dog. Repeat.

ONE REPETITION: THE DOG COLLECTS THE TOY.

Cue 'sit'. Feed the dog. Take six paces back, hold the toy out to one side and gently throw it a short distance. Return to the dog, grasp the dog's collar, point at the toy and cue 'fetch'.

Building on this game

Over time, it's better if you are less predictable in the way you play, sometimes letting the dog collect two in a row and sometimes playing a whole session where only you get to collect the toy. That way, the dog has to listen to your cues. You can also practise in different locations and gradually increase the distance between the dog and the toy.

Moving on

When your dog is keenly fetching the toys when sent and sitting calmly throughout the rest of the session, it's time to start playing the next game. But you don't need to leave this game behind; it will help improve your dog's self-control and focus. And you can revisit it whenever you want to.

Game 27:

Forgotten toys

Today's game is a simple 'memory' retrieve. The dog will see you place a toy, then be led away from it. You'll pretend to have forgotten the toy and your dog will save the day by going back to fetch it for you. It's a great game to play on walks and I'll explain how to build your dog's ability to fetch harder and harder memory retrieves.

Game goal

- Your dog will go back and collect a toy you have left behind, over a distance of up to ten paces, and deliver that toy nicely to hand.

Game overview

Like a marked retrieve, your dog will see you place a toy on the ground. But there will be a gap during which you and the dog walk away from the toy, before they get a chance to fetch it. The longer that gap, the harder the 'go-backs' are for your dog, and you'll build up your dog's memory in easy steps.

By keeping the dog at heel (on a leash if necessary) in between retrieves you'll avoid the risk of the dog making a dash for the toy as you turn to leave it behind.

Game preparation

You know the score now: toy, treat bags and long line if you need it. Attach the dog's regular leash *in addition to* this as you'll be unclipping the leash before you send the dog back for the toy.

Game steps

With the dog on a leash on your left-hand side, walk a few paces then stop.

Step 1: Circle and fetch

Cue 'sit' and give the dog a treat. Holding the leash, throw the toy out in front of you just far enough that the dog cannot reach it. Give the dog a treat. Now turn the dog in a small circle to face the toy again. Unclip the leash and hold the dog's collar. Point in the direction of the toy, cue 'fetch' and release the dog's collar. Take delivery of the toy, clip the leash back on and feed the dog. Walk a few paces forwards with the dog then stop.

There will be a gap during which you and the dog walk away from the toy. The item in my hand is the remote for the camera – not a clicker!

Step 2: Two steps and fetch

Cue 'sit' and give the dog a treat. Holding the leash firmly, throw the toy out in front of you. Give the dog a treat. Now turn 180 degrees with the dog until you are both facing the way you just came. Walk two steps then turn the dog back to face the toy. Unclip the leash and hold the dog's collar. Point at the toy, cue 'fetch' and release the dog. Take delivery of the toy, clip the leash back on and feed the dog. Walk a few paces forwards with the dog then stop.

Step 3: Ten steps and fetch

Repeat step 2 but this time walk five steps. Repeat again.

Next time you play increase to six steps, then seven steps and so on. Until your dog is able to go back for a toy after being walked ten steps away from it. Once your dog is confidently going back three or four steps for the toy, you can drop step 1.

Building on this game

This is a game that can entertain your dog under control every time you take a walk together in a safe space. You can easily build up to 50m or even 100m go-backs if you take your time and follow the principle of more successes than failures. If you build up distances too quickly, the dog may stop part-way, turn around and come back, or they might start hunting for the toy in the wrong place. If this happens walk back with the dog until you almost reach the toy and send them from there. Then, for the next few times you play, halve the distance and rebuild more slowly.

Once the dog has nailed this exercise, you can start to surreptitiously drop a toy behind you while you are walking along with the dog. Walk a few steps forwards then turn around and cue 'fetch'. Even though the dog didn't see you drop the toy, if you've played the game above often enough, the context of the walk and your cue should be enough to guide the dog to the retrieve as long as it's only about 1m away. You can then build distance with these more challenging go-backs just as you did with the previous ones.

Moving on

You don't need to build on this game in order to play the next one. You can move on to the next game as soon as your dog is reliably completing the ten-pace go-backs in step 3.

Game 28:

Lost toys

In this game you'll surprise the dog with a toy they didn't know was there. Your dog will make the awesome discovery that sometimes retrieves just happen! They'll also learn to associate the cue 'lost' with these 'blind' retrieves.

'Lost' is a cue to hunt, but implicit in that cue is the permission to retrieve. The ability to hunt with persistence is a useful skill in a dog and hunting is an activity that dogs enjoy immensely. There will be times when the toy your dog has been sent to fetch will not be thoughtfully positioned in the middle of a path. Sometimes retrieves fall into vegetation or undergrowth, or land behind a log or bush. When this happens, your dog will need to search persistently for the toy, until they find it. To build that persistence we need to give the dog lots of easy, quick wins to begin with, and introduce them to harder hunts as they grow in confidence. The lost and fetch cues are similar; what separates them is the degree of certainty.

Lost vs fetch

Both lost and fetch cues give the dog permission to retrieve. The lost cue tells the dog that there *might* be a retrieve toy or two around here somewhere so it needs to have a good search around and see if it can find one. The fetch cue tells the dog: 'If you run in the direction I am pointing, you will *definitely* find a toy.'

Game overview

In step 1 you'll leave your dog indoors, where they cannot see what you are up to, and place the toy in a fairly obvious place in your garden. If you don't have a garden and are training in a public space, you'll need a helper to hide the toy while you walk your dog in a different direction. Then you'll take your dog to the 'toy zone'. As soon as they spot the toy, you'll give your hunt cue, 'lost', and if they don't pick up the toy immediately, you'll follow it with your cue 'fetch'.

In step 2 you'll give the cue before the dog sees the toy, and in step 3 you'll make it a little harder to spot the toy, so that the dog has to search for it. And in time, your dog will start to hunt with their nose whenever they hear the hunt cue. Progress to the next step in another session, when they have mastered the previous one, rather than trying to play all three steps in the same session.

Game preparation

It's a simple game. Just make sure there are no other toys lying around outside and nothing to distract your dog in your outdoor training space.

Game steps

Leaving your dog indoors, place the toy outside in your garden, where your dog will be able to see the toy once they are within a few feet of it.

Step 1: Pairing the cue

Take your dog outdoors and cue 'lost' as soon as they make visual contact with the toy. If the dog doesn't pick up the toy immediately, take their collar, point in the direction of the toy, cue 'fetch' and let go of the collar. Take delivery of the toy, take the dog indoors and repeat until the dog is fetching the toy on the cue 'lost'.

Step 2: Using the cue

Take your dog outdoors and cue 'lost' as soon as you get into the toy zone – try to give the cue before they see the toy. If they don't start to hunt around for it, walk with them to the toy. Take delivery of the toy, take the dog indoors and repeat until the dog starts to search for the toy immediately on hearing the cue 'lost'.

Step 3: Hide the toy

Repeat step 3 but this time make the toy a bit harder to find. If the dog can't find it quickly, walk closer to it with the dog and encourage them into the area around the toy. From now on, only use the cue 'lost' for hidden toys.

As the dog gains confidence you can make the toy harder to find

Building on this game

You can build on this game by making the toy harder to find. Put it in some long grass or undergrowth, or tuck it behind a log or rock. Always take the dog into the approximate area where the toy is located. Don't expect them to hunt the length and breadth of a large garden. In advanced blind retrieving it is the handler's job to get the dog into the area of fall using whistles and hand signals. But for now, you'll just walk with your dog into the right area.

For your dog, the cue 'lost' means, 'there's a toy around here somewhere, see if you can find it'. It does not mean, 'Ha, I've hidden a toy, I bet you can't find it'. Help your dog to succeed and they'll want to play this game over and over again.

Moving on

You can move on to the next game as soon as your dog will hunt for a toy that you've previously hidden in your garden when they hear the cue 'lost'.

Game 29:

Flying toys

In this game we come back to those exciting marked retrieves again. Remember that if steadiness is important to you, you'll need to spend plenty of time on games 27 and 28.

Marked retrieves are the only way that your dog will ever become really skilled at marking, so while they should not be overdone, they are important if you are training a retriever. And they are great for building fitness as most dogs will sprint out to get that toy, and if you are lucky, they'll sprint back again too. Like any other athletic activity, it's important to build up distances gradually to reduce the risk of injury.

Getting a helper

Throughout this course I've assumed that you are training your dog on your own, but this is a game where there are great benefits to having a helper, so I'll give you two games to play: one you can play on your own and one that you can play with an assistant. The main benefit of the assistant is that it's easier to prevent the dog from being reinforced for running in if someone else is throwing the toy. If steadiness is important to you, I strongly recommend the assisted version of the game. The job of the assistant is to throw the toy and also to pick it up if the dog breaks from your side.

Game overview

You are going to teach your dog that watching a fetch toy being thrown and resisting the urge to chase it is both possible, and rewarding. In the first, and best, version of the game, you'll stay with your dog and get a helper to throw the toy a short distance from you. They'll start with short throws and build up to more exciting throws. You'll reward the dog for waiting, then send them to retrieve just as you did in the first game. Then you'll leave the dog to watch while *you* fetch the toy. This is very basic early-stage steadiness training and it's important to recognise its limitations – it will not mean you have cured your dog from chasing toys, or other moving items, in other contexts.

If you don't have a helper, you'll need to play the second version of the game where you'll sit your dog, walk several paces away and throw the toy out to one side or another. We'll build up slowly with less tempting throws first. Then you'll return to the dog, give them a treat and either collect the toy yourself or send them to fetch it for you.

Game preparation

Prepare your helper in advance. Show them where you want them to stand and where you want the toy to land. They will be throwing at right angles to the path between the two of you. Ask them not to throw the toy until you are in position with the dog sitting next to you. Explain that if the dog leaves your side before you give the fetch cue, it's their job to step on the toy and prevent the dog from picking it up. If your dog brings them the toy, they must ignore the dog completely.

Game Steps: Version 1

Step 1: Their turn

Stand next to your assistant with the dog. Let the dog see you give the assistant the toy. Walk the dog ten steps from the assistant, turn to face the assistant, cue 'sit' and feed the dog. Watch as the assistant throws the toy. Hold the dog's collar, point to the toy, cue 'fetch' and let go of the collar. Take delivery of the toy and feed the dog again.

Step 2: Your turn

Stand next to your assistant with the dog. Let the dog see you give the assistant the toy. Walk the dog ten steps from the assistant, turn to face the assistant, cue 'sit' and feed the dog. Watch as the assistant throws the toy. Feed the dog again. Now collect the toy, return to the dog and feed.

Step 3: Repeats

Repeat the game adding a greater proportion of turns for your dog if they are not excited by the game, and a smaller proportion if they seem tempted to break the sit or try to get the toy without being given a fetch cue.

Game Steps: Version 2

Step 1: Their turn

Cue 'sit'. Feed the dog. Take ten steps back and, facing the dog, gently throw the toy a short distance to your left. Return to the dog and feed. Move to your dog's right-hand side, facing the toy. Hold the dog's collar, point to the toy and send the dog with the cue 'fetch'

Step 2: Your turn

Cue 'sit'. Feed the dog. Walk 10 steps away from the dog and turn to face them. Gently throw the toy a short distance to your left. Return to the dog and feed. Walk out and collect the toy. Return to the dog and feed again. Release the dog and move on a short distance.

Step 3: Repeat

Repeat steps 1 and 2 throwing the toy to your right.

What might happen?

The dog may take the toy to the assistant. If this happens your assistant must fold their arms and look completely disinterested. They must not engage with the dog at all. You can then call the dog back to you and take delivery of the toy. Next time you play, stand much closer to the assistant and get them to throw the toy in your direction so that the dog is nearer to you than to them. You can then build back up gradually to playing further away.

The dog may run halfway and turn back. If this happens walk close to the toy with the dog and help them find it. Halve the distance between the dog and the toy in the next session.

Building on this game

Once your dog is confidently running out to the toy, and returning *to you* with the toy, you can build on this game by moving further from your helper. It's important to increase distances gradually both to keep your dog's confidence high and to avoid injury, especially if your dog runs fast each way. A good rule of thumb is to increase distances by no more than ten per cent every few days. Once the distances get greater, instead of walking out to get the toy in step 1, you can turn and walk your dog away while your assistant collects the toy.

If you don't have an assistant, one way to provide more challenging marked retrieves for your dog is with a ball launcher of some kind, and we'll look at those on page 221. You can also attach a short piece of rope to the toy to help you throw it further.

Get a helper to stand a short distance from you and throw the toy

Moving on

In the meantime, the next and final game is a great way to get your dog running longer distances without the disadvantages of using marked retrieves. You can move on as soon as your dog is confidently playing either version of the flying toys game.

Game 30:

Bucket fetch

Welcome to the final game of the book. We are not going to be fetching buckets in this game but we are going to be using a bucket to help your dog find toys as they get further away. Dogs are very good at spotting movement but if there is no movement, and a distant object does not contrast much with its background, then your dog is going to struggle to see it. It takes a great deal of confidence for a dog to run hard and fast towards an object they cannot see. If you send your dog to fetch a toy they cannot clearly see and they fail to find it that failure may dent their confidence quite quickly.

So, we help the dog win by providing them with a visual marker that tells them where the retrieve is located. In time we can dispense with the marker, but it's a great way for your dog to experience plenty of confidence-building success. All kinds of things can be used as markers, but a simple and easily available marker is a large white bucket. We train the dog to run to this marker over very short distances to begin with and increase those distances gradually. Bucket fetch is an easy game that involves running up and down and eating rewards, so it's not surprising that dogs love it!

Game overview

You'll place your bucket upside-down on some short grass or another outdoor surface where the toy can easily be seen. Later on it won't matter if the dog can't see the toy provided, they can see the bucket. To start with we must make the toy obvious too.

The game begins with memory retrieves like the ones we did in game 27: forgotten toys. The dog will watch as you place the toy next to the bucket and travel a short distance to the bucket to collect it. Once the dog associates the bucket with the toy, you can start to place the toy before you take the dog outside and later you'll gradually move the bucket further away.

Game preparation

You'll need a ten-litre white or pale bucket and your toy. Ideally, you'll have a minimum of 4–5 metres of space for the dog to run along. It doesn't need to be wide, a narrow alley between the side of a building and a fence or hedge, for example, is actually better as there are fewer distractions for the dog and it focuses the dog on the bucket at the end of the alley

When you place your bucket on the ground, the dog must be on a leash. You'll need to hold the dog (or have a helper hold the dog) so that they cannot interfere with you setting up the bucket.

Game steps

With the dog on a leash place the bucket upside-down on the ground.

Step 1: Introduce the bucket

Sit your dog facing the bucket and a few steps from it. Walk to the bucket and place your fetch toy in front of it.

Return to the dog, hold their collar, remove the leash and cue 'fetch'. Take delivery of the toy, feed the dog, cue 'sit' and place the toy in front of the bucket again. Repeat several times.

Step 2: Short bucket go-back

Walk the dog three paces from the bucket before turning them to face the bucket and sending them for the toy. Repeat at four paces, then five paces.

Step 3: Long bucket go-back

Repeat step 2 at increasing distances over several sessions, until you're sending the dog from up to 20 paces away from the bucket.

A plain white bucket is easy for the dog to see

Step 4: Bucket surprise

Leave your dog indoors or get a helper to place the bucket upside-down with the toy in front of it while you walk the dog in a different direction. Walk the dog to within ten paces of the bucket, facing the bucket, them send them for the toy.

The bucket helps to identify the location of the toy as it get further away

Building on this game

The main way to build on this game is to increase the distances over which the dog runs. Obviously, you need to consider your dog's existing fitness and health when you start to extend distances. Retrieving is more physically demanding for your dog than trotting about on a walk. Always play athletic games like these in the coolest part of the day and build up distance gradually. Check with your vet if you are in any doubt as to your dog's ability to run fast without straining muscles (including the heart) or overheating, especially if your dog is over seven years old, is very large, pregnant, has medical issues, or is brachycephalic.

Use the game to teach the dog to fetch with confidence in different environments. It's a game you can play in fields, on the beach, in parks and anywhere else where your dog is able to see the bucket at a distance. You can introduce obstacles between the dog and the bucket – a small stream or a fallen tree that the dog has to jump, for example. These need to be very easy obstacles to begin with, to make sure your dog's confidence remains high.

This is a game that can give pleasure to dogs throughout their entire life and, as the distances get greater, the benefits to their physical fitness also increase. If you are not a fan of walking around with the dog on a leash or worry about your dog getting into mischief off-leash, this game can replace some of those daily walks or simply make trips out more fun for both of you.

Moving on

Bucket fetch was the last of our 30 games. I hope very much that you've enjoyed them and that they mark the beginning of many hours of fetching and fun for you and your dog. In the troubleshooting chapter that follows I'll be looking at some of the challenges that you may have faced in a bit more depth and I'll give you some tips to help you get the best from your dog. I'll also point you in the right direction for help and support and then we'll finish up with a look at how you can take fetch further.

Afterwards

Fetch is a safe and healthy form of exercise provided you build up distance gradually

Troubleshooting

Teaching a dog to fetch in a controlled way so that retrieving can be used as a means to entertain and exercise your dog is a remarkable and highly rewarding achievement. Like many such achievements it doesn't come easily and for most of us there are sticking points along the way, and even times when we feel like giving up. So, if you need this section of the book, please don't worry; we all get stuck sometimes, and this chapter is here to help.

The two stages where you are most likely to come across those sticking points are when training the pick-up and the hold and I talk about those below. But there is also potential for problems when you move the goalposts at any point in training, including increasing distance or duration, and when training in new locations, so we'll look at ways to help you pass those hurdles too.

The pick-up

For some dogs, picking a toy up from the ground is the easiest thing in the world. With others it can take what seems like forever to get that toy into the air. If the wait is getting you down, there are several ways to try to speed things up, including:

Make the treats more interesting

Make the toy more interesting

Switch to a different toy

The 4 X 4 strategy (see page 212)

Making treats more interesting is something we often forget to do. Juicy, messy treats are often the most valuable to dogs, but you need to try out a range of tasty items to find out what *your* dog really does prefer and use that whenever you are teaching something that they find challenging.

There are a couple of ways to make a toy more interesting too. You can wrap something the dog likes around the toy, a bit of old cloth or Vetbed can work. Secure it with string or elastic bands and if this works, gradually cut away the addition once the dog is lifting the toy up. If that fails, you may need to switch to a different toy for a while. I started out teaching Polly with a white retrieving dummy and switched to her red bone toy when we got stuck during the pick-up. In fact, the main problem was not the toy, I had simply not been putting enough time into her training sessions, so I also implemented the 4 X 4 strategy (see below) and with those two changes we made a big leap forwards in our progress

The 4 X 4 strategy

The 4 X 4 approach has nothing to do with off-road vehicles. It is simply a way of reminding you to set aside four days when you know you will be able to spend four training sessions per day with your dog. We all tend to be a bit sporadic with dog training. Life is so busy and a dog training session is never urgent. Sometimes sessions get spaced out too much and there are too many days when you don't train, and it can feel like progress is very slow when, in fact, it's possible you just aren't getting enough practice in. Setting aside four days when you can commit to training several times on each of those days can give your progress a significant boost. And you'll be able to see the benefits of this more clearly if you make a before and after video of your training. Propping your smartphone up and filming yourself training can also be a great way to identify where you are going wrong!

The hold

In principle, teaching the hold should be easy. A hold is just a 'duration' behaviour like the sit-stay, or the down-stay. Once the dog will carry out the behaviour, even for just a millisecond, you ought to be able to mark it, and add duration to it in tiny increments. Unfortunately, it isn't quite that simple.

Once the dog has learned to lift the toy off the ground, what can happen is that the dog gets 'stuck' on repeatedly dropping the toy in order to get the treat. And because they drop it so quickly, you never seem to have chance to reinforce them for holding. In fact you may end up repeatedly clicking a fraction too late and reinforcing the drop itself. This is extremely common, and we really don't want it to happen because it's vital that the drop follows the release cue, not the other way around. This isn't you being incompetent, it can happen to very experienced trainers.

If you manage to avoid clicking too early, you can still have problems. It's easy to end up accidentally reinforcing the dog for throwing the toy higher and higher. This tends to happen when we withhold the click because the dog dropped the toy, which is the right thing to do, but some dogs will then offer a throwing behaviour instead. This is a mistake I made with Polly. Working on the click and catch game (see page 103) for a while is a good way to get past this, but the six-syllable technique (see below) is a great alternative. And you can also switch back and forth between them.

The six-syllable technique

Two seconds may seem like a very reasonable target to aim for when beginning the hold. But for a dog that spits out the toy the second it leaves the ground, getting to 'one thousand, two thousand' can be hard. You may need to break those four words down into their six syllables. Each of the syllables represents one third of a second.

One

Thou

Sand

Two

Thou

Sand

To begin with you may only be able to say the word 'one' in your head before you click. When your dog will hold for the word 'one' (approximately one third of a second) several times in a row you'll start aiming for 'one thou'. And so on. Building up the duration in these incredibly tiny increments is a painstaking process, but it does work! And the principle of small incremental increases in difficulty is one that you need to bear in mind throughout any dog training journey.

Increasing duration or distance

Trying to add a few more seconds to a hold or a sit can be frustrating. The tiny gains you make when using these methods can make the process seem interminable, and it's tempting to try to speed things up. But if you tried to add another ten seconds to the duration of a three-second sit you would almost certainly set your dog up to fail.

Hang on in there, it gets better quite quickly. A dog that can sit for thirty seconds can quickly and easily be taught to sit for an extra ten seconds. Probably in a single session. So when you are increasing distances and duration you need to think about adding a small percentage of what your dog can easily do, rather than a set number of seconds or paces each time you move your goalposts. It's like compound interest on your savings. As your dog's skills grow, those tiny increments get bigger and their progress gets faster.

Training in new locations

Distractions are everywhere. When you take your dog into a new environment, the chances are they won't respond in the same way to your cues, as they did in a familiar environment. And the change in environment could be quite subtle. Moving to a different part of your garden, for example, could be enough for your dog to start failing on a task you thought they had nailed down. When you change locations, there are some simple things you can do to get your dog quickly back on track and making new progress – the first is to limit your dog's options; the second is to get into the habit of purposefully engaging your dog before you begin to train. We'll look at that in a moment. The third is to backtrack a little and train at a slightly easier level. Don't worry, your dog will rapidly catch up, and you'll be ahead far more quickly than if you stubbornly try to work from where you left off in the previous location. Let's look more closely at limiting your dog's options in new locations.

Too Much Choice

Don't ask your dog to choose between playing fetch and another activity that they may enjoy even more. At least, not yet, and especially not in an environment where distractions are very appealing. Learning to focus on one game when there are other games to play is something that takes time and practice. All dogs have a hierarchy of preferences. Most dogs love to:

Chase moving objects

Sniff and follow scent trails on the ground

Play fetch

In that order. If the dog is off-leash in an open space, they may show little interest in retrieving unless you get them switched on to playing with you. Polly's preference is to sniff and follow scent trails, so if I want her to play fetch, I need to engage her in working with me first. Unless fetch is your dog's first choice, the same will apply to you.

Engagement Before Training

The key to engaging a dog in a new location is a very high rate of reinforcement and provides some easy wins for the dog. For example, I had been training Polly in my garden – on grass – and wanted to progress to training in an adjacent field where there is more space. In Polly's mind this field was a fun place to run and sniff about, not somewhere to pay much attention to humans. Polly first had to learn to walk through the gate paying me attention and staying with me. I achieved this by feeding her at my side almost constantly while walking in and out of the gate, and in small circles just inside the field itself.

If you are new to modern training methods, you might worry that you are setting a precedent that you don't enjoy. But these high rates of reinforcement are only temporary and create a mindset of focusing on you and paying attention to you. Once you have this focus and attention you can then start giving the dog some simple cues. A hand touch or a sit are a great way to start. Keep sits short, then move the dog on a few steps, feeding frequently to begin with, before asking for another sit. Start with easy wins and only add the fetch toy into the session when the dog is fully focused on working with you. Keep the 'engagement before training' rule high on your list of priorities and you won't go far wrong.

Before we finish here, let's just talk about allowing dogs to fail, because this is something a lot of us struggle with.

Allowing dogs to fail

In modern training, we go to a lot of trouble to set dogs up to win. But it's important to remember that there are times when you need to allow dogs to fail. Once of these times is when you move the goalposts. It's inevitable at this point that your dog will fail sometimes, because that's the whole point. You are raising the bar, and what was acceptable before is acceptable no longer. Usually the only way for the dog to figure this out, is to discover that they are not getting rewarded for the old standard. And as far as your dog is concerned, no reward equals a big fat fail.

For example, during hold training, when you increase the hold duration, the dog will sometimes drop the toy before they are given a release cue. This means there is no click and no reward. The idea is that the dog learns from this mistake and tries a different behaviour next time or the time after that. It may take quite a few mistakes before the dog hits on the correct behaviour, in this case, holding on to that toy a bit longer. And it's important that you don't give up during this learning period and that you don't demotivate your dog by allowing them to fail too often.

I normally recommend no more than two or three fails in a row before making the task easier for the dog. You can, however, experiment with the ratio of fails to successes. And with a well-motivated dog, you might be able to sustain their interest in the game with four or five failures in a row. This gives them more opportunity to experiment and learn from those mistakes.

Losing the collar grab

In some of our games we use restraint to prevent the dog rushing off to retrieve before the fetch cue is given. With regular steadiness practice you'll eventually be able to rely on the dog to sit still without any restraint. You can help prepare your dog for this moment when you hold their collar by waiting for them to relax and stop leaning into it, before you let go. When first practising unrestrained sits, it's a good idea to have a helper available near to the toy so that they can stand on it if the dog preempts your fetch cue.

Stop while you are having fun

Once you have finished the course, you'll want to sustain your dog's interest in the game long-term. It's important that you don't keep exceeding your dog's boredom threshold. Five minutes of play each day is a good starting point. If your dog is desperate to continue, then you can gradually increase the time you spend playing together. You want your dog to be excited when the fetch toy comes out, not thinking, 'oh dear, here we go again'. So keep fetch joyful and remember always to stop while your dog is still having fun.

Help and support

If you are a visual learner, you might benefit from watching videos of Polly playing each of the games in turn. You can find these in my FitFetch course at the Dogsnet online training school. This book is a companion to the course. You can also get support from the training team in the Dogsnet Facebook group – you'll find links to these resources on page 225.

It's worth remembering that different dogs will feel differently about playing fetch. For some it will be a just another training game that they play with you from time to time. They won't mind playing fetch, but given a choice, they might prefer just to hunt about off-leash and follow scent trails in the undergrowth. That's fine. Fetch is a useful tool to help keep your dog fit, to strengthen the bond between you and to entertain and exercise them when you don't have time for a good long walk. For other dogs, fetch will be a life-long passion: a joy that no other kind of exercise can match.

Their face will light up when they see the retrieve toy come out and you'll need to decide when it's time to quit because they would play till they drop. Whichever dog you have, enjoy them! And if you both love playing fetch, I think you'll enjoy the final chapter and finding out what comes next.

Taking fetch further

When I set out to write this book, and the video course I made to go with it, I originally planned to film one of my young gundogs as they set out on their retrieving journey. As I thought about what I wanted to achieve with this book, I realised that I wanted to show my readers is that retrieving isn't just for working labradors and spaniels – we all know they can retrieve! Instead, I wanted to show you that pretty much any dog can learn to play fetch in a way that benefits them immensely. With that in mind, I decided to train an older dog from a non-gundog breed, which is the situation many of you will find yourselves in. Instead of using my own dogs, I asked my husband if I could borrow his terrier for three months. He said yes, and Polly and I became a team.

Every dog you train adds to your knowledge. Polly has certainly added to mine and I have added to hers. Polly was four years old when we started this course. I raised her as a tiny puppy, but she has been Duncan's companion since she was six months old. And apart from keeping her recall up to scratch he has done little training with her. He used to throw the occasional tennis ball but got fed up with searching for them when she got bored with bringing them back. I started in about the same place as many pet dog owners start, with a dog that will chase a ball sometimes, but often drops it or won't give it back. The course in this book is the same course I use for my other dogs and it's the same course I am using for my youngest labrador as I write. I didn't change anything fundamental for Polly, though I have added one or two tweaks to the book in light of what Polly and I have experienced together.

What happens next?

So where do we go from here? Should I build on Polly's skills just as I would with a labrador? Or a spaniel? I haven't decided yet and I definitely need to give her back for a while to spend some quality time with her best friend. For you and your dog though, this could be the beginning of something big. There are a number of activities you can get involved with now that your dog now will fetch you a toy. Several of our gundog breeds are some of the most popular pets in the world and so I'll also talk about where I go next when I am teaching a working gundog. But before you take fetch any further, it's a good idea to look at some the safety aspects of the game, and at how you can use retrieving to benefit your dog's health.

Playing fetch safely

While fetch is an enjoyable and beneficial pastime, like so many other fun things in life, playing fetch is not entirely without risk. So we do need to talk about what the risks are, and how we can mitigate them. Obviously, a dog running around off-leash is at greater risk of accident or injury in that moment, whether they are retrieving or not, than a dog walking on a leash. But the dog that gets plenty of off-leash exercise on a regular basis is likely to be healthier in the long run than a dog that is mainly exercised on a leash. Fetch can be quite an intense form of off-leash exercise and we've talked a bit about building up distances gradually. This is important because you are building both speed and endurance during these games and your dog's muscles and cardiovascular system need time to adapt to this new form of exercise.

Remember that a dog that runs in every time you throw a toy or ball is much more likely to get hurt or to hurt someone than a dog that sits still and waits to be sent with a cue. If your dog is not steady, it's usually best to restrain them with their leash or collar while you throw a toy. You can mitigate the risks of fetch further by focusing more on blind and memory retrieves than on marked retrieves.

Some dogs will need a vet check before you take these games any further. This includes dogs with an impaired ability to cool themselves such as bulldogs, pugs and French bulldogs. Because retrieving is a demanding exercise, flat-faced breeds, dogs with certain health conditions and some elderly dogs may need you to focus on more gentle blind retrieves in which the dog is less likely to be travelling at speed. You may also need to avoid retrieving in warm weather, and you should take any other extra precautions your vet recommends.

Ball launchers

If you are anything like me, your dog will regard your ball-throwing prowess with, at best, disappointment. If you are tempted to invest in an aid to help you impress your dog with some real action, you have several choices.

A hand-held ball launcher can provide a great deal of fun. They look a bit like a plastic spoon or scoop with very long bendy handle. They are not horribly expensive, you can probably pick one up for less than £10, and they can add metres to the distance your ball travels. An electric ball launcher is a different animal. It's a battery-powered machine the size of a large pumpkin that sits on the ground and fires out tennis balls at speed. Electric ball launchers are not cheap, you won't get much change from £100 and they are not without risk.

A ball from a launcher is travelling fast and if your dog starts catching balls in the air, there is a small chance that one could get lodged in the dog's throat. I know of a dog that died this way. And although such accidents may be rare, I personally would not use a ball launcher of any kind if I could not be sure that my dog would wait to retrieve on cue. The dog tends to build up a lot of speed as soon as the ball is fired and if it overtakes the decelerating ball, the dog will spin around to pick it up. Turning at speed puts great pressure on the dog's joints. Some dogs will be able to cope with this physical strain without injury; others may not. The risks may be greater in larger dogs where the forces on the joint are greater, and in dogs such as labrador retrievers that are prone to cruciate ligament tears, especially if they are neutered. I don't want to be a killjoy here; I'm not saying, 'don't use a mechanical ball launcher,' but I am saying be careful and have your dog under control if you do. For maximum safety, it's best all round if you wait for the ball to land before you send the dog to fetch it.

Now we have got the safety issues out of the way, let's talk about what you and your dog can do with your new-found skills.

Jumping

If you'd like to be able to take photos of your dog just like the one on the cover of this book, you'll need to teach them to jump. With the exception of some very long-backed breeds like dachshunds, jumping a low barrier is safe for most healthy dogs that are fully grown. And teaching your dog to jump with a retrieve toy in their mouth is a lot of fun and not too difficult. You'll need to set up the gap you want the dog to travel through and get the dog fetching through that gap first. Once the dog is confidently retrieving through the gap you can add a small barrier. And once the dog is jumping the barrier, you can raise it. I used a couple of wooden hurdles, then added a straw bale in the middle once Polly was retrieving through the gap between them. You can improvise with items in your garden, just make sure that the barrier is soft or is very light and will fall easily if the dog bumps into it. You can buy agility jumps online that work well. To get that winning shot you'll need to lie on the ground and capture the dog as they sail over the barrier!

I used wooden hurdles and a straw bale for Polly's jump

Sports and activities

The training you have completed will have given you the skills to teach your dog anything else you dream up provided it is something that they are physically capable of and will enjoy. And there are now several other opportunities open to you. You might want to get involved in general obedience training, in working trials or in Schutzhund. And I've put links to resources where you can find out more about those on page 225. If your dog loves water, dock diving is another fun option.

If you've been bitten by the retrieving bug and own one of the sporting breeds, such as a retriever, spaniel or German short-haired pointer (GSP), then your next step to gain experience could be to join a local gundog training club. It's important to be aware that many gundog trainers are still using traditional training methods involving some force and intimidation. In some clubs you will be supported and encouraged to continue on your force-free training journey if that is what you want but not all gundog trainers will be so accommodating. If you are lucky enough to be close to a Gundog Club trainer in the UK then do take the opportunity to join in one of their classes. I am the founder of the Gundog Club and the creator of the Graded Training Scheme for gun dogs. The scheme is open to pet dogs and working dogs of any breed or crossbreed. The grades are a lot of fun to work through and all Gundog Club trainers use the force-free positive reinforcement training methods like those used in this book.

Have fun with fetch

We've now reached the end of our first retrieving journey together. I have had immense fun teaching Polly and filming our progress, much more fun than I expected. And I sincerely hope you have had fun following along and teaching your own dog this underrated and most rewarding activity. You can build on all the games in stage 6, play them often, and even invent some games of your own now. For me, the next stage with my young dogs is to teach them to stop on a whistle signal, no matter where they are, and follow my hand signals at a distance. This kind of directional control is a lot of fun to teach and I hope to be back again with *Fetch 2* so do join my email list for news of my latest books and courses.

Don't forget, it's the journey that counts, not the destination. Enjoy training your dog and pop in to the Dogsnet Facebook group if you'd like any support. I'd love to see you there!

Polly and I had such fun with these games, I hope you did too!

Resources

For further information about Pippa's online dog training courses and books visit her website: dogsnet.com.

For help and support with training your dog, join the Dogsnet Facebook group: facebook.com/groups/DogsnetTraining.

You can join Pippa's free training tips email list here: dogsnet.com/free-dog-training-tips/.

Sports and activities

The Gundog Club provides graded, positive training and tests for working and pet dogs: thegundogclub.co.uk

The Kennel Club provides a range of activities for dogs in the UK: thekennelclub.org.uk

The American Kennel Club akc.org

K9 Aqua Sports, dock diving: k9aquasports.com

Schutzhund: gsdleagueworkingbranch.com

Working Trials UK: workingtrials.info

ObedienceUK: obedienceuk.net

Pippa's online courses

All the courses below are available at dogsnet.com:

- Puppy games
- Puppy parenting
- Foundation skills
- Core skills
- Fit fetch

More books by Pippa

Total Recall
The Happy Puppy Handbook
The Labrador Handbook

Index

Note: page numbers in bold refer to information contained in captions.